The Secret Marriage of Sherlock Holmes
AND OTHER ECCENTRIC READINGS

The Secret Marriage of Sherlock Holmes

AND OTHER ECCENTRIC READINGS

Michael Atkinson

ANN ARBOR

THE UNIVERSITY OF MICHIGAN PRESS

First paperback edition 1998
Copyright © by the University of Michigan 1996
All rights reserved
Published in the United States of America by
The University of Michigan Press
Manufactured in the United States of America
⊖ Printed on acid-free paper

2001   2000   1999   1998   4   3   2   1

A CIP catalog record for this book is available from the British Library.

Library of Congress Cataloging-in-Publication Data
Atkinson, Michael, 1942–
      The secret marriage of Sherlock Holmes, and other eccentric
   readings / Michael Atkinson.
         p.   cm.
      Includes bibliographical references.
      ISBN 0-472-10710-0 (hardcover : alk. paper)
      1. Doyle, Arthur Conan, Sir, 1859–1930—Characters—Sherlock
   Holmes. 2. Detective and mystery stories, English—History and
   criticism. 3. Holmes, Sherlock (Fictitious character) 4. Private
   investigators in literature. I. Title.
   PR4624.A37   1996
   823'.8—dc20   96-10299
                                                                    CIP

ISBN 0-472-08566-2 (pbk : alk. paper)

For permission to reprint portions of some chapters, the author is
grateful to the following publishers: Bowling Green State University
Popular Press, publisher of *Clues, A Journal of Detection,* for "Type and
Text in *A Study in Scarlet:* Repression and the Textual Unconscious,"
which appeared in Volume 8, Number 1 in 1987, pp. 67–100, and for
"Virginity Preserved and the Secret Marriage of Sherlock Holmes,"
which appeared in Volume 2, Number 1 in 1981, pp. 62–70; and
Gettysburg College for "Staging the Disappearance of Sherlock
Holmes: The Aesthetics of Absence in 'The Final Problem,'" which
first appeared in *The Gettysburg Review,* Volume 4, Number 2, Spring
1991, pp. 206–14.

For all my friends
who have forgiven my love of popular culture,
and for Diane, who preferred me to Holmes.

ACKNOWLEDGMENTS

Even a slender volume such as this accumulates a pleasant stock of debts. Early and late in the process, Richard Howard provided pointed advice and astute encouragement. Jim Hall and Trudelle Thomas generously read the entire manuscript and made clear what I had not. Diane Tabachnick helped me clarify a number of stylistic and substantive points throughout the book. Among the colleagues and friends who read and commented on individual chapters, I am particularly grateful to Detmar Straub, Bob Arner, Stan Corkin, Wayne Hall, Tom LeClair, Fred Milne, and Robin Sheets. And I have benefitted from many conversations with Jon Kamholtz, who also uses Holmes in the classroom in ways quite different from mine. Victoria Gill of the Metropolitan Toronto Reference Library not only admitted me to, but actually locked me up in, their well-stocked Arthur Conan Doyle Room to do research there, while she read through some chapters in progress. Austin Wright, Rosemary Franklin, and Rosemary Herbert shone lights into the labyrinth of publication, and David Lehman opened the door to the University of Michigan Press, where LeAnn Fields, Eve Trager, Ellen McCarthy, Joseph Cislo, and Kelly Sippell have proved exceptionally congenial and helpful. With such a helpful host, even those stages of writing usually thought burdensome have proved a delight.

"There is a certain method
in the gentleman's
eccentric proceedings."

—"The Adventure of the Six Napoleons"

Contents

INTRODUCTION

*I trust that the younger public may find these romances of
interest, and that here and there one of the older generation
may recapture an ancient thrill.*
　　　　　—Arthur Conan Doyle, preface to *The Complete
　　　　　Sherlock Holmes Long Stories,* June 1929

The Secret Marriage of Sherlock Holmes is about reading, a process
that anyone who opens this book takes for granted. But Sherlock Holmes, the cultural icon to whose exploits we will give
new readings, became famous by taking nothing for granted.
His own adventures can be read in new ways, including ways
that Holmes himself would have found startling, but that can
give contemporary readers—you, I hope—satisfaction.

Even in the ordinary course of things it becomes clear
that a story supports many readings. First readings, second
readings, enthusiasts' readings, critical readings. In the chapters to follow, I will employ some of the most useful tools of
recent literary criticism, considered not as an esoteric art, but
as a set of possibilities well within the grasp of all mature
readers, not strategies to decorate texts or to prove their own
cleverness, but to enhance our enjoyment of the reading act
itself. If these tools are new to you, I hope to show how accessible they can be, and how delightful to use. If the tools are
familiar, I hope you will find them employed in provocatively
new ways to analyze these classics of popular culture.

Sherlock Holmes is the single most widely recognized
literary figure in the world—way ahead of other inquiring
minds such as Prince Hamlet or Captain Ahab—so for many,

1

reading the Holmes stories is a rereading. There are two ways
to reread. We can seek to "recapture an ancient thrill," trying
to read again as we did the first time we encountered these
tales; or we can find new ways to read, ways that bring a fresh
intelligence into play. Perhaps the best readings will be those
in which innocence and experience both have their sway, and
we can taste what it is like to "have known then what we know
now." The pleasures and insights that such a doubled reading
can bring are not limited to detective fiction, of course. But
such works provide a good place to start. Reading these mysteries can sharpen our sense of the mysteries in reading at
large.

Conan Doyle's stories themselves provide clues that lead
to new styles of reading, and if we take their suggestions seriously, we may be in for a pleasant jolt. In the 1970s, the
brilliant critic of semiotics, popular culture, and literature Roland Barthes distinguished between readerly and writerly
fiction—that which asked only our acquiescent reading, and
that which invited us to become involved in the creative process. But then he took an even more intriguing step and proposed that any text—even a well-made, traditional one—
could invite a creative, writerly response, in which we readers
take a more active role.

The Holmes tales are particularly beckoning in this way
because Holmes's own specialty is to provide a radical and new
rereading of the "obvious" and "commonplace" as well as the
puzzling. His refusal to accept the conventional meanings of
things is a chief appeal of his stories, as well as the bedrock of
his method. So he invites us to take the writerly approach to
reading.

Having brought up Barthes's name and one of his notions, I should indicate the place that critical theory will have
in this book. For academics, interest in detective fiction has
recently passed from altogether declassé to almost de rigueur,
thanks to the speculations of two French theoreticians, psychoanalyst Jacques Lacan and philosopher Jacques Derrida.
Though these *frères Jacques* have sparked a lively interest in

Poe's story "The Purloined Letter" (and by contagion other detective fiction), their own essays are largely unreadable by the uninitiated.[1] I resist the idea that thinking about popular culture becomes interesting and respectable only when the language in which it is analyzed approaches unintelligibility. Convinced that jargon is neither good language nor good thought, but often masks the lack of both, I have tried to keep technical lingo to an absolute minimum.

Beyond that, I have introduced into each chapter only the critical machinery necessary to accomplish the job I intend there. If you are familiar with critical theory, you will recognize the sources of my strategies, and don't need to be burdened by an iteration of their origins and contexts. If you are not familiar with these critical theories, you deserve to see them in action before deciding if you want to know more about them. A critical appendix has been provided if you would like to find out the theoretical roots of each chapter and be directed to a good book or two that explain that way of thinking in greater depth. (If you would like to find out more about my use of Barthes, for example, now might be a good time to have a look at the back of the book.) I hope relegating this material to the appendix will serve both kinds of readers well. Like our own biological appendices, it may be of interest to those curious about the system's inner workings, yet it can usually be safely ignored.

So, in the individual chapters, the schemes of literary criticism will serve us much as Holmes's treatise on varieties of tobacco ash or his monograph on tattoos serve in the stories: not as displays of erudition to be admired for their own sake, but as helpful systems from which we can extract what we need to illuminate key evidence. And as knowledge of tattoos may help solve one case, tobacco ash another, so our reading strategies, too, will change according to circumstance. To keep the game quick, we must be willing to be as nimble as Holmes and use what fits the case at hand.

Though there is a general progression in the following chapters from the traditionally symbolic (psychological, economic) toward the more devious and slippery (Nietzschean, postmodern), I invite you to skip around if you are so inclined, to follow your fancy or create your own sense of order. Here is a quick preview of what is to come, so you can pick and choose as you like.

Chapter 1 will examine "The Red-Headed League" to map out a range of stances we might adopt as readers—from the familiar quest to find whodunit to a bold recasting of the evidence in the manner of Holmes himself. Chapter 2 reads multiple layers of symbolism in "The Adventure of the Speckled Band" according to the philosophy of kundalini yoga. Questions of convention and formula figure in chapter 3, which shows how deeply traditional romance motifs shape "A Scandal in Bohemia," especially the conventions of preserving virginity and marrying in secret. And Conan Doyle's complex debt to Poe's conventions is the subject of the coda to that chapter that explores the relations between "A Scandal in Bohemia" and "The Purloined Letter."

Carl Jung's psychology provides a lens through which to read *A Study in Scarlet* in chapter 4, focusing not just on the characters or symbols but on the radically split form of the narrative itself. Psychological and economic symbols intersect to provide the matrix for reading "The Man with the Twisted Lip" in chapter 5. And chapter 6's reading of "A Case of Identity" combines psychology with semiotics to demonstrate that, although Holmes claims to base his approach to truth squarely on the facts, he is a actually a visionary rather than an empiricist. Just how elusive the truth can be, even for a mind like Holmes's, is the subject of chapter 7's reading of "The Adventure of the Copper Beeches," which uses both fairy tales and the deconstructive insights of Jacques Derrida to trace truth's vanishing trail.

Reversed expectations and unexpected absences are also the subject of chapter 8, which investigates the way Conan Doyle systematically inverted his own conventions to write "The Final Problem," the story in which he tried to kill off his hero. Finally, Conan Doyle's rebellion against the very conventions he is using so successfully—even as he continues to use them—suggests a Nietzschean reading of "The Adventure of the Six Napoleons" in chapter 9, which ends the book.

To read the Holmes stories from all these different angles is to realize how multiple are their sources of enchantment and power—and to realize our own versatility as readers, too. These strategies may complicate our reading, just as Holmes's views are usually more complex than those of the police; but as his thought brings us pleasure as well as clarity, so our own thoughts about him should lead to greater enjoyment and satisfaction in the end.

As you can see from the overview, each chapter treats a particular story. Though it is a rare Holmes tale that does not contain a claim for its own singularity, it is sometimes difficult to keep all these highly formulaic "singular" stories from blending together in memory. So a brief summary of each has been provided—no replacement for the suspense of the originals or the crispness (and prejudice) of Holmes's summations, of course, but a chance to recall the unembellished facts before seeing what might be made of them. As Holmes remarks in "A Scandal in Bohemia," "It is a capital mistake to theorize before one has data."

Whether you feel that these readings "somewhat embellish" the tales (as Holmes accuses Watson's accounts of doing), that they are "a little too theoretical" (as the police complain of Holmes's methods), or that (like the explanations of the master detective) they get to the truth at last, I hope the chapters that follow are persuasive enough to provoke interest, provocative enough to elicit some disagreement, and interesting enough to keep you turning the pages. *The Secret Marriage of Sherlock Holmes* is not a shotgun wedding of Holmes to a particular theory or style of reading, but a series of flirtations, tentative engagements, each with its own interest, all options kept open, hoping in the end to remain good friends with them all.

CHAPTER ONE

"The Red-Headed League": READING HOLMES WITH A HOLMESIAN EYE

"Your red-headed idea was very new and effective."

"The Red-Headed League" was one of Conan Doyle's two favorite stories, and it is easy to see why: the plot is clever, the characters are clearly etched, Holmes is performing at his best, Watson is at his most admiring, and Holmes's concluding explanation is satisfying indeed: "You reasoned it out beautifully," says Watson. "It is so long a chain, and yet every link rings true." Just to reread it as we first did can indeed "recapture an ancient thrill."

But why settle for that? To read *of* Sherlock Holmes is one thing; to read *as Holmes reads* is quite another. Rather than simply repeating the adventures of the great detective, we can solve some mysteries of our own—about the act of reading this work, and about reading itself. This story is a good place to begin because it is so rich in models of reading, models that, if not elementary, are certainly fundamental.

Most adventures in the Holmes canon begin with a visitor coming to the famous detective and putting before him the details of a story, a confusing sequence of events uninformed

---

The epigrams for various sections of this and other chapters are taken from the story under discussion, unless otherwise indicated.

by a clear meaning, in the hope that Holmes can illuminate the puzzle. So let us put before ourselves the facts of "The Red-Headed League," not just the initial dilemma or the final explanation but the whole story, and see if we can trace a pattern we didn't see before. ❧

"The course of events is certainly among the most singular that I have ever listened to."

The story itself is easy to summarize. Watson visits Holmes, who is listening to the tale of Jabez Wilson, a red-headed pawnbroker who, two months before, had been alerted to the existence of the Red-Headed League by his assistant, one Vincent Spaulding, a man so eager to learn the pawnbroker's trade that he had hired on for half the going rate. ("But after all, if he is satisfied, why should I put ideas in his head?" Wilson asks.) Spaulding was a good worker, his only personal quirk being a penchant for photography that frequently took him to the basement where he did his developing. The new assistant showed Wilson an unusual advertisement that appeared in "*The Morning Chronicle,* of April 27, 1890. Just two months ago." It offered a profitable sinecure to the right redheaded man. Spaulding encouraged his employer to apply, even guided him to the league's office, where Wilson was selected from a throng of redheads for the singular duty of copying the *Encyclopaedia Britannica* daily from ten to two, for four pounds a week. This he proceeded to do for eight weeks, only to arrive at the office one day to find the following notice tacked to the door:

THE RED-HEADED LEAGUE IS DISSOLVED.

OCT. 9, 1890.

Unable to trace his redheaded former patron (one "William Morris," for whom he has copied out articles on Abbots, Armour, Archery, Architecture, and Attica), and too disturbed about the loss of income to take the advice of his assistant to wait and see what develops, the porcine Jabez Wilson has come to consult Holmes.

The detective starts involuntarily at Wilson's description of his assistant, a small, stout man with a white splash of acid on his forehead, and satisfies himself (and us) that he knows the man when Wilson confirms Holmes's guess that Spaulding's ears are pierced. Having heard the puzzle, Holmes dismisses Wilson for the duration and takes the investigation in a direction that leads away from the pawnbroker and his petty losses. What began as the pawnbroker's story becomes the detective's.

Holmes predicts this will be a three-pipe problem; but before retiring to smoke it out, he invites Watson to join him for an afternoon concert later that day. On their way, the pair stop off in Saxe-Coburg Square, and as they stand before Wilson's shop, Holmes thumps the pavement with his walking stick. Next, he knocks on the door and asks directions from the assistant, his actual purpose being a surreptitious glance at the man's knees. Then Holmes and Watson go around to "explore the parts which lie behind" the shabby-genteel square. They observe, among the sequence of buildings along the busy thoroughfare, a tobacconist, a newspaper shop, a vegetarian restaurant, a carriage-building shop—and a bank.

At the concert, sure that Holmes is doing serious mental work while apparently only listening to the music, Watson reflects admiringly upon the "dual nature" of his friend's genius. Holmes is by turns "smiling, . . .languid, [and] dreamy" or "relentless, keen-witted, [and] ready-handed"—at some times "poetic and contemplative" and at others an exemplar of "brilliant reasoning power." The concert over, they agree to meet at ten that night. Watson is to pack a revolver against potential danger (and, of course, for heightened suspense).

At ten, Watson reaches Baker Street to find Holmes with the fundamentally stupid but reliably tenacious Inspector Jones, accompanied by a phlegmatic Mr. Merryweather, the chairman of the bank whose back abuts the pawnshop. That bank is now host to some thirty thousand napoleons of French gold. Merryweather feels certain the gold is safe and repeatedly laments missing the pleasure of his customary rubber of whist in order to admit the foursome to the vault, though Holmes assures the banker that he "will play for a higher stake tonight" than at his usual Saturday night card game. Once in the cellar, Merryweather proclaims the soundness of the vault, tapping its floor with his cane. The floor rings as hollow as his boast.

Having confirmed that the bank's security is undermined, Holmes remarks that this foursome will not have the chance to play whist tonight, though he had brought a pack of cards. They darken the lantern and sit down in the obscurity to await the arrival of the felons. Holmes's announced mission is not just to safeguard Merryweather's gold, but to deliver into Inspector Jones's hands a nefarious criminal—the fourth smartest man in London, John Clay (aka Vincent Spaulding). In just over an hour's time, light peeps forth as John Clay chips his way through the floor to carry out the theft and is apprehended by Holmes. Clay's companion flees to the tunnel's other end and into the waiting arms of the law.

In an oddly memorable moment, Clay compliments Holmes on the deftness of the capture, and Holmes compliments Clay on the cleverness of the crime. And as Jones handcuffs him, Clay disdainfully insists on being addressed as nobility, a whim the inspector indulges as he leads his "highness" off to jail. Accepting Merryweather's thanks, Holmes confesses he had old scores of his own to settle with Clay, and is also glad to have heard the story of the Red-Headed League.

Back at Baker Street, Holmes explains to Watson what was obvious to the master detective from the first. As he read the events, the league was no more than a ruse to clear Wilson from the premises, invented by the assistant, who secured his place in the shop by working for half wages. His frequent visits to the cellar implied tunneling, a deduction supported by the worn knees on his trousers. The solid tap on the sidewalk in front of the shop meant that the cellar (and thus the tunnel) went behind it instead, confirmed by the presence of the bank on the thoroughfare directly behind the pawnshop. When the tunnel was fully opened, the league was closed, and the robbery promised to take place on Saturday night, leaving all Sunday for undetected escape. Hence Holmes could know the crime, the place, the time. Watson praises Holmes's virtue as benefactor to mankind, but Holmes graciously avers it was but an escape from ennui for him—as it has certainly been for us. ✤

> *I trust that I am not more dense than my neighbors, but I was always oppressed with a sense of my own stupidity in my dealings with Sherlock Holmes. Here I had heard what he had heard, I had seen what he had seen, and yet from his words it was evident that he saw clearly not only what had happened, but what was about to happen, while to me the whole business was still confused and grotesque.*

Now that we have seen the facts of this fiction, how do we read them? The story itself provides a gallery of different reading styles—styles that we can recognize, examine, or even adopt.

Chances are we do not read as Jabez Wilson does, though we may be tempted to in our more indolent moments. The pawnbroker is the most unreflective of what Roland Barthes calls "readerly" readers. His responses are completely predictable: he is pleased at the advertisement's promise, angry at the dissolution announcement, and diligently oblivious as he copies. Wilson is quite satisfied to undergo a certain amount of ennui to gain modest, predictable rewards. Four pounds a week is enough to keep him at his desk, dutifully copying facts from the *Encyclopædia Britannica* in the order they appear, repeating exactly what he reads, without question. He is readerly

reading at its dullest. He corresponds to that tendency everyone feels sometimes to read docilely, taking what is given, just
as it is given. Finding out whodunit is the modest payoff we are
willing to settle for in this frame of mind. But this story offers
other, more interesting models of reading.

Since Watson is the narrator of most of the stories, we
read *with* Watson—as well as often reading *as* Watson reads.
With Watson we listen to the facts Jabez Wilson presents, and
with him we condescend to this "obese, pompous and slow . . .
commonplace British tradesman." With Watson we admire
Holmes's ingenuity, having faith it is there when we cannot
see it, and praising it when it is made clear in the final revelation. Even as we read with Watson, we can see his limitations, of course, often picking up clues before he does
(singling out the bank as significant among the buildings
behind the pawnshop, for example). We can see Watson himself and be touched or amused at his devotion to Holmes or
his conviction that his friend is "a benefactor of the race."
Reading with Watson does not mean being confined to his
vision.

To read *as* Watson reads is to appreciate Conan Doyle's
craft just as Watson appreciates Holmes's—to follow admiringly in the author's footsteps. We are both more aware
and more humble than the Wilson-like reader who concludes
"there was nothing in it after all" when Holmes reveals his
methods. Like Watson, we are aware that there is something
about the genius of the creator that always eludes us. We infer
the cast of Conan Doyle's mind from repeated exposures to
his work, as Watson at the concert can give a portrait of
Holmes's mentality based on their long association. We are
willing to forgive, even treasure, Conan Doyle's little lapses
and eccentricities. In this mode, our reading is admiring, attentive, loyal. As Watson does not take the initiative but follows
faithfully, we are content to be good readerly readers, quite
satisfied to "recapture an ancient thrill," responding as Conan
Doyle seems to have intended us to, following his directions as
Watson follows Holmes's, admiring the craft by which we are

led. It is a satisfying way to read. But not so satisfying as becoming Holmesian readers. ❃

> *I took a good look . . . and endeavored after the fashion of my companion to read the indications.*

What would it mean to read as Holmes reads? In the first place, we should become a little suspicious of the readings already given. Holmes does not discard the facts Wilson brings him, but he does not trust the pawnbroker's interpretation of the events. *To read as Holmes does, then, would mean to doubt Holmes's account of his story's significance as Holmes doubts Wilson's.* Holmes's doubt does not just lead him to add missing bits and pieces here and there, to complete the picture Wilson originally drew. The shift is much more profound.

Holmes's reading of the case amounts to a Copernican revolution. The mystery no longer revolves around Wilson and the league but Clay and Holmes himself. He dismisses Wilson and his interpretation of the events; Conan Doyle even puts the pawnbroker to sleep during the climactic action. In a bold stroke, Holmes shifts the center of the puzzle from the league's office to a tunnel between the pawnbroker's basement and the bank. Wilson's absence, not his presence, is the key. A minor character (Spaulding) becomes major (Clay), and what began as the pawnbroker's story of profit and loss becomes the story of Holmes settling old scores.

Here, in this shifting of the mystery's center, is the key to Holmesian reading, and the basis for the rest of this book. Holmes is an active and powerful reader. He makes the case his own by recentering the narrative. His reading is ec-centric, and our pleasure is rooted in his eccentricity. Eccentricity is not just an endearing collection of quirks adorning Holmes's celebrated logic. It is the essence of his method, the heart of his strategy.

Rather than merely admiring that eccentricity, we can become eccentric readers ourselves, discovering unexpected connections and finding new layers of significance among the

familiar materials of these adventures. (Already we have begun to read eccentrically by focusing on this story as a gallery of reading styles.) As an eccentric, Holmes takes pleasure
in operating a little outside the law, "intrigued by all that
is bizarre and outside the conventions." Our own investigations get more intriguing, and our enjoyment can be multiplied, when we do the same, reading these stories not as examples of the conventions of the detective genre, but outside
the confines of those laws. We might notice, for example, the
marks and traces of other genres that wend their ways through
a tale such as this, leaving their tracks like footprints in soft
earth.

We could begin our discoveries where Holmes begins his.
The first shock of recognition ripples through this story when
the detective recognizes something in Jabez Wilson's description of Vincent Spaulding: "a white splash of acid upon his
forehead." Upon hearing this, "Holmes sat up in his chair
with considerable excitement." Do we? Do we come to attention or smile with pleasure when Holmes asks if the
man's ears are pierced, and Wilson replies that they are? While
Holmes is recognizing Clay, we can recognize this ancient
device of recognition itself. Recognition by scars was already
old when Odysseus's aged nurse spotted the scar on his thigh,
when Oedipus looked down anew at his own pierced ankles,
when Cain wandered the earth with his marked brow, or when
Thomas touched the wound in Jesus's side.

So as Holmes recognizes an old acquaintance, so do we—
a device that Aristotle duly cataloged more than two millennia
ago. Alerted by the acid splash on Spaulding's forehead,
Holmes asks about other marks—pierced ears. We, too, can
ask how many familiar marks of myth this story bears. Here
before us is the ancient tale of the hero who descends to the
depths, wanders through a labyrinth, and finds a treasure—a
tale as old as Jason and the Argonauts, or Jonah and the whale,
Beowulf, or Hansel and Gretel—all done up in Victorian
guise. Here too, as we will see shortly, are traces of the brother
battle, ancient as Gilgamesh, when Clay and Holmes, two intel-

ligences without moral anchors, face one another at the juncture of bank vault and tunnel. And here too is the hero's clever defense of the weak old king's treasure.

Like the scars on mythic heros, these marks of myth in the detective story can be hidden, but not erased. Reading this relatively new fictional form, we can experience with pleasure the shock of the old, if we are willing to read eccentrically, stepping out of the narrow confines of the genre to see the myth behind the tale, the bank behind the pawnshop.

That link between bank and pawnshop—so laboriously dug, so cleverly screened—suggests another eccentric reading. Holmes typically claims that his own untainted rationality is as free from economic concerns as from social mores. He often (as here) rises above fees and works simply for the challenge, to dispel ennui and "escape from the commonplaces of existence." But to take Holmes at his word would be to read the tale "centrically," like Watson, accepting the master's estimate of himself at face value. If we read instead as Sherlock Holmes does and doubt Holmes's account as Holmes doubts Wilson's, his proclaimed independence from the economic and political system and his condescending distance from Merryweather look as suspicious as Spaulding's offer to work cheap.

The whole structure of the story is economic, and Holmes is deeply implicated. To Holmes it may seem merely incidental that the building providing access to the bank is a pawnshop; but we can see it differently. Just as the three gold balls on the crest of a Renaissance banking family, the Lombard Medicis, eventually came to mark the poor man's substitute for a bank, so Merryweather the banker and Wilson the pawnbroker, each oblivious to the other, are more linked than they know, as the subterranean landscape suggests.

At both ends of the tunnel, we might ask who employs whom? Wilson is glad to exploit his new employee, keeping him in the dark so he will work for half wages. But of course it is instead Clay who employs Wilson in his designs; and he contributes rather generously to the pawnbroker's support, even as he mocks him with meaningless work. At the tunnel's other end, Holmes declines any fee, explaining he has employed this occasion to trap an old enemy, Clay. But we can see how thoroughly he is employed by the banker and the whole system of capital, to the defense of which he leaps so automatically that his own proclaimed independence is mocked. It is ideology, not collusion, that puts Holmes in the service of the banker. As surely as Clay supports the pawnbroker at whose gullibility he must smile, Holmes unhesitatingly springs to support the conventional world from which he claims such distance.

From an eccentric standpoint Holmes appears very centric indeed, and his claims to be free of the social order ring as hollow as Merryweather's boasts that the floor of the vault is sound. Though he would deny it, Holmes is as much a tool of Merryweather as Wilson is a tool of Clay. ❦

"You seem to have done the thing very completely. I must compliment you."

"And I you," Holmes answered. "Your red-headed idea was very new and effective."

To question one of Holmes's eccentricities is not to dismiss them all. Holmes calls attention to his own amorality when, rather than vilifying the villain, he compliments Clay on his ingenuity. As the men exchange civilities, it becomes clear that they complement as well as compliment each other. Detective and criminal present moral mirror images, a fearful symmetry. The common Clay, his forehead symbolically scarred, reflects reason disfigured, yet insists on his nobility; Holmes's lofty brow remains unwrinkled as he insists on the absence of noble motives, claiming to have solved the crime just to settle an old score and drive off ennui. They are like men of ancient myth, discovering in the heat of battle that they are brothers.

Here at the tunnel's mouth, there opens beneath us an abyss that is often in the neighborhood of a Holmes story, the chasm that separates rational thought from moral feeling, an ethical hollowness that echoes throughout the canon. It is not merely a question of Holmes identifying with the antagonist in order to solve the crime. Holmes invites us to tap him and find him ethically hollow. He has no moral center to distinguish him from Clay. He floats free of the ethical pieties Watson embodies. The detective and criminal are closely and curiously linked here by their lack of ethical center and their mutual respect. And of course Holmes's existence as a detective—his very essence—depends absolutely on the criminal: no crime, nothing to detect. The brighter the criminal is, the more brilliant the detection can be. For Holmes to find the tunnel, Clay had to dig it—and to envision the league and Wilson's hours of obedient reading.

The reader's relation to the writer is close kin to the detective's relation to the criminal. Both detective and reader rely entirely on the criminal for the pleasure of their pursuits. Like Holmes, how can we help being obliged to Clay—and to Moriarty, Moran, Roylott, and the young Rodger Baskerville? We are grateful to Conan Doyle for spawning this nefarious multitude, as Holmes is grateful to the criminals for helping him escape boredom. It will not seem too eccentric, I hope, if we take Holmes's words to Clay and recenter them, directing them to Conan Doyle: "Your red-headed idea was very new and effective." As the reader is something of a detective, the author is curiously like a criminal, hatching plots for us to solve. Without his machinations the whole elegance of detection, and the pleasure of reading, would collapse. Recognizing the link between writer and criminal may give us a startle, as Holmes was startled to recognize that the "innocent" Spaulding was actually Clay, but the writer is the chief plotter in each adventure, and it is his designs we seek to understand—though not to thwart.

As a plotter, the writer has much in common with the criminal. He must construct his plan, set his bait, and keep his secrets. Clay seized brilliantly on the fact that his accomplice and the man he needed to dupe both had red hair. Connecting this correspondence in a new way, he elaborated the entire fiction of the Red-Headed League. Arranging the facts to correspond in new ways is the essence of plotting. As the action unfolds, the meaning changes. The insignificant becomes significant in light of later revelations; one person's story becomes another's; the casual becomes the causal; the irrational is revealed to be reason itself.

Like Clay, Conan Doyle has designed an artifice that at first dazzles us, but that we are later to see through—though not before experiencing its power and charm. For a plot exists to be experienced, not just to be known. When we speak of the plot's rising action, its building tension, climax, falling action, and resolution, we are of course actually speaking of different moments in our responses as readers. When the plot thickens, it is actually the reader's sense of connections and correspondences that grows denser. Details become clues, and with clues we solve the mystery, explaining the puzzle of events we began with.

Readers, like detectives, respond to plots by active plotting of their own, pointing out new connections and correspondences so that new meanings emerge. What intrigues reader and detective alike is unraveling one plot and (re)constructing another, either as a "readerly" reader duplicating the detective's discoveries or as a "writerly" reader, seeing what the detective (and perhaps the author) did not.

Plotting to get beneath the plot is the very subject of "The Red-Headed League." As we know from real estate and cemetery maps, a plot is a piece of ground, as well as a map to describe it. And this is a tale about Holmes's making a mental plat map (that is, a plot map, a land diagram) to survey the shape of things beneath a plot of ground, Saxe-Coburg Square. We aim to find out what goes on beneath the plot and behind the facades of the facts we first see—here, the facades of the pawnshop and bank as well as the duplicitous facade of the league and the impassive face of the reasoning Holmes. The underground connections that relate all these appearances and give them new meaning constitute the deeper plot, or plan, of the story.

So as active, eccentric readers we share in the "criminality" of the author; we plot our own course through the fictional landscape and infer the existence of secret tunnels that link the trivial to the treasured, pawnshops to banks, enabling us to pull off what Eliot called "raids on the inarticulate," revealing what the story does not speak about itself. And like the detective, we recreate the criminal's plot but give it a different outcome, making a plot of our own. We can enjoy ourselves most if, as Holmes did with Clay, we can take pleasure in the author's skill and still be willing to catch him in, and learn from, his mistakes. ❈

"I shall keep piling fact upon fact on you, until your reason breaks down under them and acknowledges me to be right."

Mistakes? Clay's mistake—dissolving the league a little too early—gave Holmes the chance he needed to see the elegant design and purpose of the Red-Headed League. Conan Doyle's mistakes are equally revealing, and like Clay's, they turn our attention away from the ostensible show and recenter our interest.

Conan Doyle may have tipped his hand when he made Wilson—that dogged copier of facts—so unlikable. Facts were of little consequence to Conan Doyle. He could not keep them straight; he was indifferent to details. In writing this story— one of his favorites—Conan Doyle made two slips so elementary even Watson should have spotted them, not to mention Holmes.

We can be more observant. It might take more than one reading to notice that the address of "the offices of the League" is first given as 7 Pope's Court, and later as number 4. But the confusion of dates is harder to miss, especially since it is twice reiterated. At Holmes's direction, Watson makes a note of the date the advertisement for the Red-Headed League appeared: "*The Morning Chronicle,* of April 27, 1890. Just two months ago." And Wilson notes that "eight weeks passed" in his job at transcribing before he came to the offices to find the sign proclaiming:

THE RED-HEADED LEAGUE IS DISSOLVED.
OCT. 9, 1890.

It is an odd calendar indeed that finds only eight weeks, two months, between April 27 and October 9. It will hardly do to say that Wilson was enjoying himself and time passed more quickly than he thought, or that in a mystical moment, the fiction has transcended the bounds of space and time. The true puzzle is not Conan Doyle's initial carelessness, but the fact that the error stood in edition after edition of this story Conan Doyle took such pride in, and stands in all editions today.

So facts, at such a premium for Holmes, are mere distractions for Conan Doyle. In a curious sense, author and criminal agree in their methods: Clay keeps Wilson's nose at meaningless facts, and Conan Doyle suggests the pleasures of detection lie in paying more careful attention to detail. But the real action is elsewhere, in the changing moods and shifting imagination of the great detective (and of the Holmesian reader). As Watson marvels during the concert, "The swing of [Holmes's] nature took him from extreme languor to devouring energy," from "extreme exactness and astuteness" to a "poetic and contemplative mood." Holmes's great liberating talent is to be fickle, mercurial—fickle enough to switch allegiances in "A Scandal in Bohemia," mercurially swinging from cool professionalism to volatile outrage and back again in "A Case of Identity," both of which we will look at in later chapters.

Now languorous, now vigilant, now the artist, now the scientist, Sherlock Holmes is a man of many allegiances as well as many moods, all of them temporary. He is burdened by no such consistency as he condemns in the police, who repeat the same methods of investigation in case after case. In one story he will claim axiomatically that it is the featureless, commonplace crime that presents the greatest difficulty, in another that a crime's singularity is its challenge.

Unlike many eccentrics, he is not frozen into a singleness of mind. He is passionate and playful, focused and fickle by turns. Amoral, he can admire intelligence where he finds it. Operating a little outside the law, he is neither captive of its conventions, like the police, nor pitted against it, like Clay, who in being an outlaw—"murderer, thief, smasher, and forger"—is as much subject to the law in his way as the police are in theirs. Holmes is not illegal, just unlawful—inconsistent, elusive, hard to pin down.

Can we be as intelligently fickle, as astutely faithless as he? It is a tall order. For us, that will mean invoking many different styles of reading, rather than "proving" that a psychological or a deconstructive reading provides a universal fit. Eccentric readings should not all be of the same cut; Holmesian eccentricity is not a new habit but rather an escape from habit, a willingness to experiment. And the most pleasing eccentric reading would never lose contact with the surprise and delight of our naive readings. For the aim is not to destroy the conventional reading, but to complement it, enhance it with new pleasures.

Holmes's relation with Merryweather makes the point. To drive away his ennui, Merryweather counts on playing whist. He expects a game in which all the rules are laid out, as we do when we pick up a Sherlock Holmes story looking to "recapture the ancient thrill." Holmes promises Merryweather, "[Y]ou will play for a higher stake tonight," and will he or nill he, Merryweather is won to Holmes's less commonplace way of finding excitement.

But then a curious thing happens. As Holmes and Mer-

ryweather sit in the vault together with Watson and Inspector
Jones, Holmes speaks:

> "I am afraid . . . . we must put the screen over that dark
> lantern . . . . and sit in the dark. . . . I had brought a
> pack of cards in my pocket, and I thought that, as we
> were a *partie carrée*, you might have your rubber after
> all."

It is a consummate Holmesian move, for it implies that
Holmes had not only taken the trouble to learn Merryweather
regularly played whist on Saturday nights, but was actually
prepared to join him in enjoying the diversion, if circumstances permitted. For Holmes, two kinds of pleasure seeking
can meet and become a third.

Can we guess the style of pleasure Holmes anticipated in
playing whist sitting just above the tunnel, the abyss? Certainly
the impending robbery would add a certain sauce to the game.
Barthes calls sustaining two apparently contradictory pleasures "perversion," a rather Gallic way of noting we can maintain multiple attitudes in the same reading moment—from
the familiar willing suspension of disbelief to the more esoteric deconstructive turn. The chapters that follow will propose different Holmesian readings, recenterings of the stories
they treat. But in each case, the new, Holmesian perspective
can exist in a fruitful tension with Wilsonian or Watsonian
readings. For as Holmes himself demonstrated when he came
prepared to play a round of whist, even while awaiting the
arrival of the bank robbers, we can have our gold and rubber
too.

CHAPTER TWO

THE SUBTLE SERPENT IN "The Adventure of the Speckled Band"

"The idea . . . was just such a one as would occur to a clever and ruthless man who had had an Eastern training."

Asked to name his favorite Sherlock Holmes tale, Conan Doyle couldn't remember the title and called it simply "the one about the snake." That story was "The Adventure of the Speckled Band," and most readers favor it as well—with good reason. Conan Doyle was thoroughly right to call it "the one about the snake," for the story touches just about every form the serpent takes in our conscious and unconscious imaginations. His forgetting the title, too, was "right"—for it points us toward the reason Holmes at first failed to comprehend the significance of those mysterious words, "the speckled band," and then toward the curious way in which Holmes at last came to grasp their meaning.

With the passing of time, the title may not be the only feature one forgets, even in so vivid a tale as this, so here is a review of the salient details. ❧

Working as he did rather for the love of his art than for the acquirement of wealth, he refused to associate himself with any investigation which did not tend towards the unusual, and even the fantastic.

Of all Holmes's cases, Watson "cannot recall any which pre-sented more singular features" than this one. "It is possible that I might have placed them upon record before, but a promise of secrecy was made at the time, from which I have only been freed during the last month by the untimely death of the lady to whom the pledge was given."

The adventure begins when that lady, a young but graying Helen Stoner, arrives shaken at 221-B Baker Street. She has heard that Holmes "can see deeply into the manifold wicked-ness of the human heart," and she comes to seek his help in resolving fears that even her fiancé dismisses as "the fancies of a nervous woman."

She has good cause for fear. Her stepfather, Dr. Grimesby Roylott, is a violent-tempered physician who once beat his native butler to death while serving in India. There he also married the recently widowed mother of two-year-old Helen and her twin, Julia. Shortly after the family returned to his ancestral home in England, Helen's mother was killed in a railway accident, leaving Dr. Roylott in charge of her consider-able fortune until such time as the girls might marry. The grounds of their remote estate are now oddly populated with living memoirs of India—a cheetah and a baboon—as well as a troupe of wandering gypsies who have become the hot-tempered Roylott's only associates.

Two years earlier, Helen's sister Julia had accepted a pro-posal of marriage, and her stepfather raised no objection. But a fortnight before the wedding, she died. The night of her death, Julia had complained to Helen of the scent of cigar smoke from Roylott's adjacent room, and she reported hear-ing a low, clear whistle for the previous three nights. Later, both girls locked themselves in their respective rooms (as one would on an estate hosting wild animals and gypsies) and retired to sleep.

Helen heard the "wild scream of a terrified woman," and as she opened her door, she "seemed to hear a low whistle, such as [her] sister described, and a few moments later a clanging sound, as if a mass of metal had fallen." Her sister's door opened, and Helen saw Julia fall to the ground in convulsions, shrieking "O, my God! Helen! It was the band! The speckled band!" and pointing toward the doctor's room. Dr. Roylott arrived on the scene, administered brandy and summoned further medical aid from the village, but all efforts to revive her were in vain. Julia's demise was all the more mysterious because the room was sealed tight, there were no marks of violence on her body, and the village coroner could detect no trace of poison. "It is [Helen's] belief that she died of pure fear and nervous shock, though what it was which frightened her I cannot imagine."

Helen's life has disturbing parallels to her twin sister Julia's. She, too, has recently become engaged, and, though her stepfather again offered no opposition to the match, he undertook house repairs that required Helen to put herself in a very uncomfortable position:

> my bedroom wall has been pierced, so that I have had to move into the chamber in which my sister died, and to sleep in the very bed in which she slept. Imagine, then, my thrill of terror when last night, as I lay awake, thinking over her terrible fate, I suddenly heard in the silence of the night the low whistle which had been the herald of her own death.

Holmes agrees the matter is most urgent. Both he and Helen suspect the band of gypsies. Before they can leave for the estate, Holmes and Watson are confronted in their Baker Street rooms by Dr. Roylott himself, who has come to warn the pair not to meddle in his affairs. He demonstrates the strength of his rage by seizing the poker and bending it with his bare hands. Though Holmes, not to be bested, nonchalantly straightens the poker out again, it is clear Roylott is a dangerous character.

Holmes and Watson leave for the estate, posing as architects. They agree the repairs are just excuses to move the young lady from her room. Trying the shutters from outside, Holmes discovers they cannot be forced and must discard his initial theory that gypsies entered the room from without. Inside the fatal room, noticing the bed is clamped to the floor, Holmes focuses on the "bell-rope which hung down beside the bed, the tassel actually lying upon the pillow." He is told the bellpull was "only put there a couple of years ago." With a brisk jerk, Holmes discovers it is a dummy. "The rope—for so we may call it; since it was clearly never meant for a bell-pull," was "fastened only to a hook just above . . . the little opening of the ventilator"—also installed just two years ago, shortly before Julia's death.

The investigation proceeds to Dr. Roylott's room, in which Holmes takes note of a large metal safe, a saucer of milk, and a dog lash tied in a loop. Holmes explains that when night falls he and Watson will wait outside for Helen to signal that Roylott has retired. Then they will take her place in the fateful chamber, while she goes to her own proper room, even though it is in disrepair. Clearly Holmes thinks the danger lies not outside the house, but within. Soon the signal lamp gleams, and they advance. Just before they enter the window, "out from a clump of laurel bushes there darted what seemed to be a hideous and distorted child, who threw itself on the grass with writhing limbs, and then ran swiftly across the lawn into the darkness." Watson, like the reader, is struck by the full horror of the image, which Holmes only partly dispels by explaining that what they saw was a baboon.

In the fatal room, they keep a dark and silent vigil. At last they hear a low whistle.

> The instant that we heard it, Holmes sprang from the bed, struck a match, and lashed furiously with his cane at the bell-pull. . . . [H]is face was deadly pale, and filled with horror and loathing. . . .
> Suddenly there broke from the silence of the night the most horrible cry to which I have ever listened. It

swelled up louder and louder, a hoarse yell of pain and fear and anger all mingled in the one dreadful shriek. . . .

"What can it mean?" I gasped.

"It means that it is all over," Holmes answered.

Entering Roylott's room, they find him sitting quite dead beside the open safe, the dog lash in his lap.

Round his brow he had a peculiar yellow band, with brownish speckles. . . .

"The band! the speckled band!" whispered Holmes.

. . . In an instant his strange head-gear began to move, and there reared itself from among his hair the squat diamond-shaped head and puffed neck of a loathsome serpent.

"It is a swamp adder!" cried Holmes "—the deadliest snake in India. He has died within ten seconds of being bitten. Violence does, in truth, recoil upon the violent."

Using the dog whip as a noose, Holmes replaces the serpent in the safe and closes the door. The terrified Helen is sent off to "the care of her good aunt at Harrow," and police are left to infer that the doctor died while "indiscreetly playing with a dangerous pet."

Holmes admits he was led down the path of error by the presence of the gypsies and Julia's peculiar use of the word *"band."* When he realized the apparent bellpull was just a rope, the idea of a snake instantly occurred to him—a source of a poison so exotic as not to register in the tests of a country coroner. The snake was trained to return to the sound of a whistle and fetch its reward of milk, and the metallic clang was the sound of the closing safe that served to cage the serpent. Every night the doctor "would put it through the ventilator . . .

with the certainty that it would crawl down the rope, and land on the bed. It might or might not bite the occupant, perhaps she might escape every night for a week, but sooner or later she must fall a victim."

Attacking the serpent with his cane, Holmes drove it back through the ventilator and "roused its snakish temper, so that it flew upon the first person it saw. In this way I am no doubt indirectly responsible for Dr. Grimesby Roylott's death, and I cannot say that it is likely to weigh very heavily upon my conscience." ❀

> *"The idea of a snake instantly occurred to me, and when I coupled it with my knowledge that the Doctor was furnished with a supply of creatures from India, I felt that I was probably on the right track."*

Since this is "the one about the snake," it will pay to have a closer look at that serpent. In concocting a snake that responds to a whistle (snakes are deaf), drinks milk (at the very bottom of a serpent's dietary choices), climbs both up and down ropes (!), and produces a venom that kills in ten seconds if the victim is male and immoral, several minutes if she is female and innocent (whereas the fastest death caused by any known species of snake is measured in hours, no matter what your mother told you)—in concocting such a snake, Conan Doyle reveals himself to have skipped the research in writing his favorite story.

Nor did Holmes himself consult (or write) an expert's monograph on herpetology to clarify the case. That has not, however, prevented many readers from essaying naturalistic speculations of their own. After reviewing the possibilities exhaustively, *The Annotated Sherlock Holmes* concludes, "It would seem, regretfully, that *no known species of snake fully satisfies all the requirements of 'the speckled band.'*" But finally, with an eloquence striking for one whose tongue is lodged firmly in his cheek, the editor endorses this possibility:

> the creature was a horrible hybrid, bred by Dr. Roylott—a sinister combination of the Mexican Gila monster *(Heloderma horridum)* and the spectacled or Indian cobra, now known as *Naja naja naja.* It would have fangs in the upper jaw inherited from one parent, and in the lower jaw from the other, and a venom incomparably strengthened by hybridization, thus assuring the almost instant demise of any victim. Here we have an animal . . . with ears like any lizard, wherewith to hear a whistle; and one whose legs and claws permitted it to run up a bell-rope as easily as down.[1]

Admirable as we may find such ingenuity, it may be more to the point to put the Indian cobra's name into the language of the gila monster's Mexico and call it *nada, nada, nada*—an airy nothing, a fine hippogriff, a worthy entry in imagination's bestiary. Conan Doyle shut his eyes to facts and concocted an outrageous beast that could do *his* bidding as well as Dr. Roylott's, one that could assure that violence would punningly "recoil" upon the violent.

Now since this is literature, not natural history, and since, as Aristotle reminds us, art is more philosophical than history, we would do better to look to philosophy for the nature of this snake. Conan Doyle made it an Indian snake, so we quite naturally turn to Indian philosophy. Conan Doyle had Holmes see a snake where others saw only a rope, and that almost gives the game away. Here is how the famous trope is put in one of yogic philosophy's central texts, Shankara's celebrated *Crest-Jewel of Discrimination:*

> For example, [in the moonlight] you see a rope and think it is a snake. As soon as you realize that the rope is a rope, your false perception of a snake ceases, and you are no longer distracted by the fear which it in-

spired. Therefore, the wise man who wishes to break his bondage must know the Reality.[2]

In this story of things Indian transported to English soil, Conan Doyle uses the well-known Indian formula by reversing it. Like the meditating yogi, Holmes keeps a still and silent vigil to await his revelation. But whereas the Indian sage sees what looks like a snake and knows it to be just a rope, the great detective sees a "mere" rope and knows it will bear a snake. The result of this knowledge is not to banish fear, but to increase the shudder of terror we feel. In short, the Indian wisdom is present, but, like a proper yogi, stood on its head.[3]

Roylott committed his crime by bringing an Indian serpent to England. Utilizing the time-honored method of identifying with the criminal's mind in order to resolve the case, I would like to follow Roylott's lead and import to the good English soil of the Holmes canon another distinctively Indian serpent to do some work for me—to indicate how *many* manifestations of the serpent turn up in this story and give such power to "the one about the snake." Using the arcana of Hindu philosophy in the way Holmes employs treatises on tattoos and deep-sea fishes to clarify his cases, I would like to introduce the fabled kundalini serpent into this reading of "The Adventure of the Speckled Band."

Classical yogic philosophy envisions the mystical kundalini to be a serpent of subtle substance lying coiled inside the base of the spine, from which position it can be roused, through meditation, to move up through and to awaken the seven chakras, or energy centers, positioned along the spine at different levels of the psychic body. These centers represent different physical and psychological energies, as well as a sequence of distinct ways of viewing any reality. Here is a little schema of the chakras, their corresponding bodily areas, and the styles of outlook associated with them, moving traditionally from the bottom up.

At the lowest—the anal—chakra, one simply holds on to the necessities of life, grasping and hoarding, never letting go. Here, the human spirit is shrunk to its most constricted. The

7 Sahasrara (crown chakra): transcendent enlightenment
6 Ajna (third eye chakra): compassionate wisdom
5 Visshuda (throat chakra): articulation, discrimination
4 Anahata (heart chakra): healing, reconciled dualities
3 Manipura (navel chakra): ego identity, willed action
2 Svadisthana (genital chakra): sexuality, procreation
1 Muladhara (anal chakra): hoarding, retention

FIG. 1. THE SEVEN CHAKRAS OF KUNDALINI YOGA
Illustration: Marion Cosgrove

second chakra, associated with the genital region, sees everything in sexual terms. Don Juan and Freud live here, and some
students think their English professors do too. The third
chakra, located in the navel region, is the center of ego and
identity. At its best, this center is represented by the questing
hero who defines a new identity by undertaking adventures.
The fourth chakra's name is Anahata, literally "no hit" or "not
striking." Here opposites are unified and reconciled, healing
the divisions that tear at the heart. At the throat is the fifth
chakra, articulation and purified discrimination. Here, one
can not only see things as they are, but speak them as well. The
famous third eye is the sixth chakra. From its vantage, one sees
with complete compassion and wisdom. And the seventh
chakra, at the crown of the head, represents the opening of
the mind to cosmic consciousness, beyond the mundane experience of everyday life. As the yogi purifies mind and heart, the
energy represented by the kundalini serpent moves up the
chakras, shifting the concerns of life upward, from just holding on to what one has, toward opening to the fullness of the
divine.

For centuries these centers, through which the subtle energy of the kundalini ascends, have represented stages of spiritual evolution. They can also help us to read literature more
richly. For each story, even each image, can be seen from these
differing perspectives, considerably enhancing our reading.
Take the literary and mythological image of the serpent itself.
At the first chakra lies the dragon serpent who guards the
treasure hoard and holds the maiden captive. The second
chakra gives us the familiar phallic serpent of Freud. At the
third chakra, the hero's emerging identity is well imaged by
the snake shedding its skin. The serpents winding up the physician's staff or caduceus embody the healing spirit of the
fourth chakra. At the fifth chakra, discrimination is the key,
and one is able to distinguish snake from rope, illusion from
reality. We are wise as serpents, if not as gentle as doves. The
serpent of the Ajna chakra (or third eye) is strikingly embodied in the cobra who peers from the forehead of the pharaoh's
crown. And the seventh chakra is well represented by the great

hooded serpent who rose above the Buddha to shelter him during the storm preceding his enlightenment.

It is remarkable how many of these serpents figure in "The Speckled Band" and amplify its power. Let us have a look, taking the second chakra first.

A snake is certainly a most unusual murder weapon, but it is more than that. Dr. Roylott's unsettling ingenuity suggests a motive scarcely to be measured by the simple desire to preserve his ancestral estate. If on the conscious level this is a story of a stepfather who wants to retain control of his stepdaughters' fortunes, at the unconscious level we have a picture of the father who simply wants his daughters. (Physically, Helen bears the marks of abuse: the doctor's grip has left bruises on her wrist. In Conan Doyle's original manuscript, Helen Stoner was Helen Roylott and Dr. Roylott was her natural father.)[4] This subliminal incest theme is one of the things that makes us uneasy as we read. Certainly the image of a (step)father penetrating the walls of his daughter's room so as to slip his serpent in has both the power and the indirectness to activate our response without awakening us entirely to what is there. We see the rope and not the snake, as it were, and yet we find it disturbing. The same is true when Holmes and Watson glimpse what seems "a hideous and distorted child, who threw itself on the grass with writhing limbs"—a nightmare vision of incestuous offspring, realistically explained away as a baboon, after its unsettling impression has been made.

It takes only a shift of perspective (from the second chakra to the first and the third) to see here the clear outline of heroic romance, traditionally typified by St. George and the dragon. The first, or anal, chakra is the home of the tyrant holdfast and the hoard-guarding dragon. Dr. Roylott is the retentive tyrant who holds the maiden and the money captive in the wasteland, and the swamp adder is a miniature of the dragon-serpent who guards the treasure. Its lair is a metal safe, no less. With his faithful companion Watson, Holmes is the knight errant who risks his own life to do battle with the dragon and rescue the maiden, wriggling out of a near-death situation, once again to establish his particular heroic identity.

The other chakras, and their serpentine representatives, play roles here as well, though perversely. Rather than holding up the serpentine staff of the physician, Dr. Roylott manipulates his snake with a whip. He has abandoned the art of healing and taken up the cruel science of poisons. At the adventure's end, the striking image of the snake's head rearing out from his hair presents a gruesome parody of the sacred cobra head that gazes out from the pharaoh's crown. Here is wisdom gone awry, caught in a grotesque image that stays with us long after we close the book. The life-giving third eye of wisdom has become the vacant stare of death.

The seventh, all-protecting serpent of enlightenment quite transcends any heights this story might reach, even subliminally, and so it is absent. But the fifth chakra of discrimination and articulation, distinguishing snake from rope and eloquently elucidating the mystery, is the presiding genius of this tale, well embodied in the measured phrases of Holmes explaining all at the story's end.

Though Holmes himself would likely have shrugged off comparisons to the dragon slayer, the path of the kundalini makes clear just how richly and variously the serpent archetype and its associated characters manifest themselves here. To reduce a story like this to mere iterations of old patterns would be a mistake, but to miss the serpent's diverse archetypal presences would be to ignore a significant source of the tale's vitality—a force so compelling that we are quite willing to overlook all the contrivances and loose ends and fall gladly under its spell. ✤

> "I had," said he, "come to an entirely erroneous conclusion. . . . The presence of the gipsies, and the use of the word 'band'. . . were sufficient to put me upon an entirely wrong scent."

Conan Doyle too was under the spell of the serpent, as his faulty memory reveals. To cast the snake into the formula of a

Sherlock Holmes adventure, he had to put it into a puzzle that the intellect could solve. So Helen Stoner brings Sherlock Holmes a rational puzzle—a classic sealed-room mystery—accompanied by a verbal clue, Julia's dying phrase: "It was the band! The speckled band!" But years later, recalling the powerful climactic scene in which the innocent-looking rope conveys the venomous snake toward the waiting detective in the dark of night, it is no wonder that Conan Doyle forgot the word *band*—such an improbable word for serpent, at least as contrived as the talents the snake required to enter and leave the apparently sealed room. The word itself left no mark on its author. It faded like the setup of a joke too intricate to remember.

Holmes himself does not solve the mystery of the word *band* in language, but by a series of migrations. His understanding of the word, like ours, goes through several turns: the group of gypsies, the gypsies' headdress, and only finally (and most improbably) the snake. Significantly, his understanding changes only as he himself changes positions in the story—a strategy that is deeply appropriate to a story in which so many things migrate, taking one another's places. Dr. Roylott takes the place of Major General Stoner, the late husband and father, and then moves the family from India back to England. After his wife's death, Helen and Julia replace their mother as Roylott's access to wealth. Within the manor, Helen fears that by moving to Julia's room she will take her sister's place as a victim as well.

Holmes's migrations begin when he steps into the role Helen's fiancé should play, believing in the young woman's fear and coming quickly to her aid, even spending the night in her room. At the climax, he stands in for the intended victim of the crime. In taking Helen's place, he also "becomes" Julia, waiting in her room, immobile on her bed, striking a match as she did, seeing the same snake she saw, and finally speaking her very words—"the band! the speckled band!" Only then does he understand. Holmes, often so oracular himself, is here perplexed by oracular words until he has moved through the spaces and confronted the images that give the words meanings, images that linger long after the words have ceased to puzzle. Like Oedipus wandering the circuit of Corinth, Delphi, and Thebes—the round of son, stranger, and husband—Holmes decodes the prophecy not as a sequence of words to be defined, but as a series of roles to be taken on: fiancé, sister, victim. He cannot investigate the mystery lexically; he must live it out. Confronting the speckled band, he too experiences the terror: he is "deadly pale, and filled with horror and loathing."

Holmes's migration does not stop with his taking the victim's place. He moves through the role of villain as well. When Dr. Roylott visited Baker Street and bent the poker in a show of strength, Holmes was quick to step into his place and bend the poker back again. In the end, rousing the snakish temper of the swamp adder and driving it back through the ventilator, Holmes is as much a killer as Roylott, as he admits to Watson. No wonder he is content to mislead the police about how Roylott came to be bitten by the snake: in covering the doctor's crime, he covers his own.

The path to Holmes's understanding the word *band* is as sinuous and changing as the route of the kundalini serpent itself. Contrary to the image Holmes cultivates as the detached investigator, here he does not stand inviolate, a Cartesian experimenter untouched by what he contemplates. Victor, victim, and villain, he is thoroughly involved, even implicated, in the crimes. ❧

> *"It is not cold which makes me shiver," said the woman. . . .*
> *"[I]t is fear, Mr. Holmes. It is terror."*

Conan Doyle uses a host of means to make sure the reader, like Holmes, experiences the frightfulness of the crime as well as the elegance of its solution. The very distance and coolness that Holmes abandons, Conan Doyle gives to Roylott, who stands outside the scene he would affect. The image of detached reason he presents is chilling. It makes his crime all the more unsettling. As Holmes puts it, "When a doctor does go wrong he is the first of criminals. He has nerve and he has knowledge." A violent man who has turned all his strength to cruel calculation, Roylott is all the more frightening in his restraint. Constructing his elegant plan, letting a snake do his work for him, he presents us with a demonic mirror of the detachment we usually attribute to Holmes (and thus fore-shadows the archvillain Moriarty). The patience with which Dr. Roylott put the adder down the rope night after night, waiting until it chose to strike, is a sinister version of the charged vigils Holmes keeps in this and other stories. Knowing of the snake's nightly visits (as Julia and Helen did not), we shudder at the peril to which such innocents were repeatedly exposed. Roylott's clamping the bed to the floor intensifies the sense of immobilized helplessness we feel for his victims. When, upon reflection, we realize that since killing Julia, he has for two years kept the snake in readiness for Helen, his coldness of mind seems all the more horrible.

In addition to the disturbing strategies of the doctor, Conan Doyle increases the story's sense of fear by charging the other characters with it as well. Fear has already shot gray through young Helen's hair, and her firm belief that fear itself killed her sister only adds to the general atmosphere of gothic terror. To increase the shudder brought by Roylott's death cry—a "hoarse yell of pain and fear and anger all mingled in the one dreadful shriek"—Conan Doyle makes it a haunting part of the region's folklore: "They say that away down in the village, and even in the distant parsonage, that cry raised the sleepers from their beds."

These sympathetic resonances of fear combine with the many forms of the serpent archetype to make this one of the most exciting and memorable adventures, and they keep our understanding of the mystery, like Holmes's, from being merely intellectual. As the speckled band moves through the shadows and slithers down the bellpull toward Julia, toward Helen, toward Holmes, that serpent can be fully understood only when it gives a shudder to detective and reader alike. ❈

> *"Hum!" said he, scratching his chin in some perplexity, "my*
> *theory certainly presents some difficulties. . . . I can only*
> *claim the merit that I instantly reconsidered my position. "*

Arriving at the meaning and experiencing the frisson of "the speckled band" are so satisfying that Conan Doyle can leave the original purposes of the investigation dangling. After all, Holmes takes on Helen Stoner's case to save her life and free her to marry. Yet at the end of the story, she is packed off to the care of her "good aunt at Harrow" with not a word of fiancé or marriage. What's more, Watson frames the tale by saying that Helen's untimely death has at last freed him to tell it, but leaves us ignorant of how she met her premature demise just a few years after Holmes saved her from being killed. It may be that ragged stories are best served by eccentric readers, willing to shift ground as the opportunities arise, gypsies like those that thread their way through this adventure.

Holmes himself is something of a gypsy here. Erroneous as well as errant, Holmes first suspects the "band" of gypsies, then says his "only . . . merit" is that he was quite ready to change his mind, abandon his position. So, as we move through these stories, we too can be willing to camp for a while in Hindu or Nietzschean philosophy, in psychology or economics, deconstruction or myth, not seeking a final destination, a conclusive style of interpreting to call home. Like the gypsies who come to town, or the knight errant of romance who stands behind the figure of Sherlock Holmes, we will live off what we find at hand when we arrive.

Certainly it would be folly to cling to the stories' much advertised logic. A close, well-illuminated look is fatal to that illusion. As Holmes discovered the danger of an innocent bellpull—seeing the snake rather than the rope—so we find that these detective stories are more slippery, more interesting and more dangerous to our settled ideas than we had imagined—which is perhaps the first and final lesson of "the one about the snake."

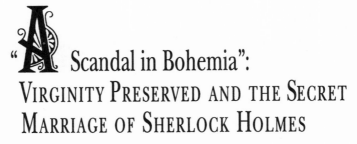 "A Scandal in Bohemia": VIRGINITY PRESERVED AND THE SECRET MARRIAGE OF SHERLOCK HOLMES

(WITH A CODA ON POE'S "The Purloined Letter")

"Your Majesty. . . . Was there a secret marriage?"
"None."

For addicts and aesthetes alike, and even for the casual reader, the very conventionality of detective fiction is one of its most enduring delights. With each adventure of Sam Spade, Lew Archer, or Jane Marple, the pleasure increases as we recognize and come to expect the repeatable, the characteristic, the formulaic: the impossible puzzle, the careful review, the knowing silence, the courtroom scene, the deft explanation. Discriminating and demanding as music critics hearing a new sonata, we listen for the repetitions, the set pieces, in which Philip Marlowe, Nero Wolfe, and Perry Mason address the world, its crimes, and their own companions, drawing pleasure from new articulations of the form, variations on the theme.

Certainly Conan Doyle's Sherlock Holmes stories are rich in this pleasure, structured as they are around the initial Baker Street interview, the investigation of seemingly unrelated data, and the concluding revelation—all studded with Holmes's spectacular readings of surface details, Watson's reminiscences and astonishments, and the pair's brisk repartee. Reading these stories we sense we are near the fountainhead of detective fiction, the source that Nero Wolfe mimes, Hercule Poirot parodies, and the hard-boiled shamuses revise. But if the detective tradition stretches forward to this day, it also reaches backward in time, toward romance.

Many detective stories are romances in disguise, and if we read them eccentrically—according to the conventions of romance, rather than those of the detective story—we find fresh pleasures and insights. Take the case of "A Scandal in Bohemia." Here is a story that shows a different face when we read it with an eye to one of the most familiar stock conventions of literary and popular romance—preserving one's virginity under siege.

The story is a curious one, and so is the convention I propose to point out, so we should take a few minutes to recall the outlines of the plot. ✳

"It is a capital mistake to theorize before one has data."

Introducing this, the famous detective's first adventure in short-story form,[1] Watson announces he is going to tell us the story of "*the* woman" in the life of Holmes, a confirmed bachelor and disdainer of both women and the softer passions they evoke. Watson, himself recently married and thus parted from the company of Sherlock Holmes, is returning from a professional call when he passes before the Baker Street window and sees his old friend's pacing silhouette. Hungry for contact with the sleuth's penetrating mind, Watson ascends the stairs and enters. In a quick top-to-toe, Holmes's searching eye reads the changes that marriage and return to medical practice have made in Watson. Then, together they turn their inferential powers on a letter Holmes has received, deducing from its paper and syntax that the writer is wealthy, German speaking, and Bohemian—conclusions he confirms when he arrives and announces himself to be Count von Kramm, a pseudonym as obvious as the black mask he wears, both of which he drops when Holmes addresses him frankly as the hereditary king of Bohemia and asks him to state his case.

The problem is vengeful blackmail, or so the king claims; its form, a picture from the past showing his majesty in the company of "the well-known adventuress" and opera singer from New Jersey, Irene Adler. She now purportedly threatens to prevent his marriage to the Swedish princess Clotilde (or any other woman, save herself) by sending the compromising photograph to the princess or to her parents on the day the betrothal is to be announced, three days hence. Quizzing the king to make sure he has tried all methods, persuasive and forceful, to recover the photo, Holmes agrees to retrieve the picture and rescue the king. He pockets Adler's Serpentine Avenue address along with a thousand kingly pounds for three days' operating expenses, asking Watson to return the next afternoon to lend his ear and his aid to the progress of the case.

Shortly after the appointed hour, the waiting Watson is startled by his friend, who enters the Baker Street flat costumed as a stablehand, "a drunken-looking groom." He quickly changes to his customary tweeds and, after collapsing limp with laughter, recounts the events of the day. Disguised as a "groom out of work," Holmes had descended to Serpentine Avenue and inspected Adler's home, noting its door lock, window fasteners, and other second-story possibilities. Currying the favor of the neighborhood stablehands, he took his fill of gossip concerning Miss Adler, her habits, and her single male visitor, Mr. Godfrey Norton, whom he shortly watched arrive at the lady's lodging, expostulate with her excitedly, and dash off in a cab, shouting to the driver his goal—to reach St. Monica's Church by noon, only twenty minutes away. No sooner had his cab disappeared than Irene Adler shot from the door, revealing in a glimpse her smiting loveliness ("a face a man might die for," Holmes says). She, too, jumped into a carriage, her aim and urgency the same as Norton's—and as Holmes's, whose commandeered cab follows suit. Once in the church, intending to spy on the ceremony from the safety of distance and disguise, Holmes was summoned from the shadows to play official witness to the event, taking away a bemused smile at his role and a gold sovereign in token of the bride's favor and thanks.

Undeterred in his mission, even spurred by this unsuspected turn of events, Holmes secures Watson's promise of help in the next act of the drama, then disguises himself as an "amiable and simple-minded Nonconformist clergyman" and directs their steps to Serpentine Avenue to enact a ruse in which Irene Adler herself will show him the hiding place of the photograph. Shortly, she arrives and several (Holmes-hired) hangers-on vie to help her from her carriage, the competition for a copper quickly becoming a brawl. Holmes, as clergyman, feigns to rescue the lady from her distress but is himself apparently wounded, then carried into her house and laid on the couch from which he signals for air. When the window is opened, Watson, as arranged, throws a cigar-shaped smoke bomb through it and raises a cry of "Fire"—though not without qualms, as he too has been struck by the beauty (and the kindness) of Irene Adler.

Smoke fills the room, and moments later, Holmes's voice is heard assuring all it was a false alarm. Rejoining Watson at the corner, he explains the working motive of the ruse as they walk home. The scuffle of the hirelings and his pretended injury got him into the house where, at the threat of fire, he might watch Adler dash to the location of her most valued possession—the photograph, hidden in a recess behind a sliding panel in the sitting-room wall. It remains only for the king, Holmes, and Watson to call on Irene Adler early on the morrow. Shown to the sitting room to await the lady, the king can have the pleasure of seizing the photograph with his own hands, and the trio can disappear with the evidence before she descends to meet them. The plan explained, Holmes and Watson have reached Baker Street, when a "slim youth in an ulster" who had hurried by bids "Good night, Mr. Sherlock Holmes" in a voice that the detective knows he has previously heard but cannot place.

The next morning, as the trio proceeds to her home, Holmes reveals to the king that Adler has married, thus removing the threat of an exposure that would now harm her as much as him. The relief of the king is combined with a possessive stab of regret that this fine woman was not of his station and thus could not be queen. They arrive to find the lady fled; *they* have been tricked, not she. Plunging his hand into the hidden recess, Holmes pulls forth a letter addressed to him from Adler, explaining how she had seen through Holmes's disguise and ploy—and even donned male disguise herself to follow him home, confirm his identity, and bid him good night. She has left the country, and she keeps the photograph—not to wrong the king, who is free to act as he wishes without hindrance from her, but to protect herself from any future royal moves against her.

Beside the letter to Holmes, she leaves for the king a souvenir photograph of herself—posed alone. But it is Holmes who covets the photograph, preferring it to the emerald ring the king offers in payment (though Holmes does retain the thousand pounds the king advanced him). The king readily yields the picture, though he reiterates his regret that Adler was on a different level from himself. "She seems, indeed, to be on a very different level to Your Majesty," Holmes echoes, in a cold and condescending sneer at the king and all he stands for. The detective even ignores the extended royal hand as they part. And that, Watson tells us, is how "the best plans of Sherlock Holmes were beaten by a woman's wit" and how Irene Adler acquired, in Holmes's life, the "honorable title of *the* woman." ✥

"Kindly look her up in my index, Doctor," murmured Holmes.

It is a good detective story, and, in its own repressed way, a good romance. And if we recenter our reading of the story around the romance convention of virginity threatened and preserved, we will find an unexpected dividend, even though in this marriage-filled story, virgins may at first seem a little hard to find.

The defense of virginity assailed from all corners is of course a central theme of romance, popular and classical, ancient or modern. From the *Odyssey's* Penelope and the Bible's Susanna and the elders, through Isabella in *Measure for Measure,* to the dauntless leading ladies of novels that sell briskly from the grocery store book racks, the woman defending her beleaguered chastity against all comers is a theme so crucial to romance that it seems to lie at its very core. But how does it function in "A Scandal in Bohemia"?

On two counts, it may at first seem odd to think of Irene Adler as someone defending her virginity. First, no matter how firmly our sympathies may finally come to rest on her side, she is presented by Watson on the story's first page as "Irene Adler, of dubious and questionable memory," and the Bohemian king labels her a "well known adventuress" with no dissent from Holmes or Watson. Both the king and Holmes, who so quickly enters his service, cast Irene as the aggressor. It is she who threatens the king and not the other way around—or so they would have it. But right from the start, the evidence of the story runs counter to these defamations of her character. Follow the curve of this early dialogue and watch the fun of the repartee turn a little sinister, even though Holmes continues to smile.

> "Your Majesty, as I understand, became entangled with this young person, wrote her some compromising letters, and is now desirous of getting those letters back."
> "Precisely so. But how—"
> "Was there a secret marriage?"
> "None."
> "No legal papers or certificates?"
> "None."
> "Then I fail to follow Your Majesty. If this young

person should produce her letters for blackmailing or other purposes, how is she to prove their authenticity?"

"There is the writing."

"Pooh, pooh! Forgery."

"My private note paper."

"Stolen."

"My own seal."

"Imitated."

"My photograph."

"Bought."

"We were both in the photograph."

"Oh, dear! That is very bad! Your Majesty has indeed committed an indiscretion."

"I was mad—insane."

"You have compromised yourself seriously."

"I was Crown Prince then. I was young. I am but thirty now."

"It must be recovered."

"We have tried and failed."

"Your majesty must pay. It must be bought."

"She will not sell."

"Stolen, then."

"Five attempts have been made. Twice burglars in my pay ransacked her house. Once we diverted her luggage when she travelled. Twice she has been waylaid. There has been no result."

"No sign of it."

"Absolutely none."

Holmes laughed. "It is quite a pretty little problem," said he.

That Adler, not the king, is the one being besieged certainly becomes clear from this early interchange. And we are also witness here to Holmes's good-natured acceptance of the siege and his easy enrollment as its agent. But if it is clear that she is besieged, is it clear that she is a virgin? Such a claim seems odd, even outlandish, when speaking of a woman who was the king's mistress, however much we might be inclined to discount the description of her as a "dubious and questionable . . . adventuress." Yet traditionally virginity has been a social, religious and literary condition, rather than a strictly biological one. The priestess prostitutes in the temples of Ishtar were forbidden to marry and were thought of as sacred and eternally inviolate by those who lay with them. More pertinently, if the long list of besieged virgins in literary romance includes such biological virgins as Shakespeare's Isabella and Jane Eyre, also included in the pantheon are Penelope, the biblical Susanna, the Duchess of Malfi, and Hester Prynne. Critic Northrop Frye has gone a long way toward explaining the development of this convention of romance.

> In the social conditions assumed, virginity is to a
> woman what honor is to a man, the symbol of the fact
> that she is not a slave. . . . A woman deprived of her vir-
> ginity, by any means except a marriage she has at least
> consented to, is, to put it vulgarly, in an impossible bar-
> gaining position.[2]

Indeed, it is precisely her independence, her freedom to consent to a marriage of her choice, that Irene Adler seeks to maintain in protecting the symbol of her virginity—a bit of film hidden in a recess of her sitting room—even though the photograph paradoxically depicts, or implies, a scandalous liaison.

For the king, too, "virginity" is directly translatable into freedom of action, its loss into bondage. After all, the entire adventure is driven by the King's attempt to restore his own appearance of chastity, which he claims his former mistress threatens. If he wishes to marry the Scandinavian princess Clotilde, he must be immaculate, or at least free of other entanglements; she will not wed a man of stained reputation.

Yet virginity has more than a domestic use, does more than guarantee a free marriage choice. Frye, still discussing feminine virginity, takes us another step of the way we need to go:

The social reasons for the emphasis on virginity, . . .
symbol of the heroine's sturdy middle class independence, . . . however obvious, are still not enough for
understanding the structure of romance. . . . With the
figure of Rebecca [in Scott's *Ivanhoe*], the innocent victim of a venomous bigotry who remains steadfast in her
faith, we begin to see that romance, in its stress on the
theme of virginity, may be talking about something
more than the condition of the hymen membrane. . . .
Deep within the stock convention of virgin-baiting is a
vision of human integrity imprisoned in a world it is in
but not of, often forced by weakness into all kinds of
ruses and stratagems, yet always managing to avoid the
one fate that really is worse than death, the annihila-
tion of one's identity.[3]

These words help us understand the seriousness of Irene
Adler's defense of her own virginity and freedom by any available means. By keeping the photo, and by marrying a man of
her own choosing, she struggles to preserve her own identity,
the humanness of her being as a person, rather than accept
the role of the king's cast-off whore.

Sherlock Holmes himself is the most notable virgin in the
story, and we can use Frye's insight to arrive at a better understanding of the detective's situation as well. For it is Holmes, as
fully as Adler, who is the victim of the king's assault—precisely
in being its agent. It is *his* integrity that is nearly made the
king's prisoner: only at the end does Holmes rescue his own
integrity and moral independence. It is Holmes, nearly cor-
rupted, who emerges inviolate, frostily repulsing the king and
dispelling his power.[4]

Holmes is, of course, a virgin on the literal level as well,
the only one in the story. And his biological virginity, too, is
threatened, or at least tested. Watson opens the story by contrasting his newly married state with Holmes's resolute bach-
elorhood and his congenital distaste for the fair sex, to which
this episode provides the single and enduringly memorable

exception. Watson is at pains to depict his friend as a scoffer at women's wit and a disdainer of the softer passions, of which he never speaks "save with a gibe and a sneer." Even as he introduces the story in which his friend is once and for all so captivated by Adler that forever after "to Sherlock Holmes she is always *the* woman," Watson takes care to stress that

> it was not that he felt any emotion akin to love for
> Irene Adler. All emotions, and that one particularly,
> were abhorrent to his cold, precise, but admirably bal-
> anced mind. He was, I take it, the most perfect reason-
> ing and observing machine that the world has seen; but
> as a lover he would have placed himself in a false
> position.

Watson later suggests it was admiration for her wit, nothing more, that provided the charge for Holmes's attraction. But Holmes's own words of description, uttered before any demonstration of the lady's wit, open other possibilities. "I only caught a glimpse of her at the moment, but she was a lovely woman, with a face a man might die for." Now this could conceivably be a report of what "a man"—any man save Holmes?—might feel, but it almost certainly expresses the degree to which he himself was personally struck.

So, we have it both ways, simultaneously: she is *the* woman of his life, and yet he loves her not—or at least will not admit it. This emotional tension or ambivalence is central to the pleasure of the story, and to its eccentric connection to the tradition of romance. "A Scandal in Bohemia" is a favorite of Holmes devotees and of casual readers alike because it provides a story in which Holmes's vigilant virginity is at once sustained and relaxed. His disdain for women and for the pulse of passion seems to evaporate in the warmth of his admiration for Adler, yet he himself makes her marriage to another man possible, in that very act denying her forever to himself. This is the stuff of purest romance, chivalric or domestic, medieval or modern. Holmes scarcely need yield to Sidney Carton in *A Tale of Two Cities* or to Bogart's Rick in "Casablanca."

Holmes must preserve his virginity, for reasons that the romance tradition makes clear. Like Galahad and the other Grail knights, he draws his power (specifically his power to *see*) from his purity. Holmes is grounded firmly in the long tradition that sees male chastity as a source of heightened abilities. As warriors (and boxers) withdraw from the women of the tribe before battle, as Catholic priests maintain celibacy in order to administer the sacraments, as Polynesian fishermen and Pueblo hunters spend chaste nights of ritual and concentration before seeking their prey, so Holmes depends on chastity for his logical acuity. Physical passion would be a debilitating impurity in his nearly superhuman sensibility. Watson puts it this way:

> Grit in a sensitive instrument, or a crack in one of his own high-power lenses, would not be more disturbing than a strong emotion in a nature such as his. . . . For the trained reasoner to admit such intrusions into his own delicate and finely adjusted temperament was to introduce a distracting factor which might throw a doubt on all his mental results.

Mind holds complete sway over matter for Holmes. It is the intellectual challenge that quickens his lust, his insight that is penetrating, and his explanations that satisfy so completely. Sexually, Holmes remains pure, and therefore powerful.

Yet, of course, it is precisely his giving up Irene Adler that allows her to be forever *the* woman. She passes into the realm of the ideal. Holmes is eternally monogamously faithful to Adler, captured in the chaste ideality of the photograph she left to the king as a consolation, an image more valuable to Holmes than kingly (or matrimonial) rings. Even "when he refers to her photograph, it is always under the honourable title of *the* woman." In short, his sustained physical celibacy is accompanied by a spiritual marriage—a marriage right before us in the text, if we will look again, and this time follow Holmes's advice and observe as well as see. ✽

It was not merely that Holmes changed his costume. His expression, his manner, his very soul seemed to vary with every fresh part that he assumed.

Where are we to find this invisible event? By looking at what is already before us. There are a number of disguises in the tale. Rather than automatically looking behind the disguises, let us look *at* them, and see what the surface phenomena tell us. (Certainly the king's disguise reveals some truth about him even as he hides behind it. Masked, he pretends to be a count, less than a king; ethically, he proves to be less than kingly in his selfish, unyielding assault on Irene.) We know that Holmes's role as the witness to the marriage enables Irene Adler to become Irene Norton (though Watson pointedly preserves her maiden name throughout the narrative). But how do the detective's roles in disguise enable her to become *the* woman for Holmes?

Let us look at his disguises themselves. There are two. In his first, he is "a groom out of work"—a stablehand, of course; but surely his presence at the wedding in groom's guise asks us to consider the other, matrimonial, meaning of *groom* as well, a meaning that stands quietly in the shadows, like Holmes himself, waiting to come out and bear witness. And do we not smile in recognition as we watch Holmes respond to the ceremony in this light?

> I was half dragged up to the altar, and before I knew where I was, I found myself mumbling responses which were whispered in my ear, and vouching for things of which I know nothing. . . . It was the most preposterous position in which I ever found myself in my life.

A state of mind many grooms might privately confess, I suspect.

If a wedding requires a bride, a groom, and a witness, it also requires someone to solemnize it. And in a coincidence now not altogether remarkable, we remember that Holmes's final disguise, the one that allows him entrance to the lady's house, is the garb of a "Nonconformist clergyman" who, on the pretext of coming to the lady's aid, actually seeks access to her couch and glimpses the recess in which her secret is hidden. Thus the pattern is complete. Playing all the roles a male could play—witness, groom, and clergy—Holmes has facilitated two weddings: one, though hasty and private, a matter of public record; the other, so secret the bride is not aware of it (as is the case with so many fancied liaisons). Yet she acquires by it an "honorable title" as *the* woman in Holmes's life.[5]

In a Freudian mood, we might speculate about the tale's final disguise—Irene Adler's appearance in male costume, as a slim youth whose voice Holmes of the faultless memory cannot recognize, even though he heard it close up that very day. We might reasonably ask whether this, in connection with Adler's combining "the face of the most beautiful of women, and the mind of the most resolute of men" hints at the reason that "as a lover, [Holmes] would have placed himself in a false position." But hints of homosexual leanings, as disquieting to himself as to his author and his public, provide a less comprehensive and ultimately less satisfying explanation for Holmes's position than do the literary traditions of romantic devotion to the ideal and male virginity as a source of superhuman power.

This combination of overt chastity and an ideal marriage in disguise is simply the literary and symbolic extension of what makes this story such a favorite in the first place. It captures for us, in multiple exposure, an enduring moment when integrity is threatened and vindicated; when virginity is relaxed and preserved; and when Holmes's purity is tested and emerges firmer, because tempered, alloyed, and strengthened with a trace of something else. This is the key to the tension and the pleasure the story offers us—the struggle and the triumph of romance.

ODA: "A Scandal in Bohemia" AND "The Purloined Letter"

*"It is simple enough as you explain it," I said smiling. "You
remind me of Edgar Allen Poe's Dupin. I had no idea that
such individuals did exist outside of stories."*

*Sherlock Holmes rose and lit his pipe. "No doubt you
think that you are complimenting me in comparing me to
Dupin," he observed. "Now, in my opinion, Dupin was a very
inferior fellow. . . . He was by no means such a phenomenon
as Poe appeared to imagine."*

—A Study in Scarlet

What are promises for, if not to break occasionally, and better
sooner than later? Although this book is based on strategies of
reading the Holmes canon eccentrically—outside the conventions of detective fiction—still, the fame and recent academic
respectability of "The Purloined Letter" and the quite peculiar
link between Poe's story and "A Scandal in Bohemia" make it
impossible to resist tracing the connections between them.

Conan Doyle's debt to Poe was no secret. He listed the
American as a major influence and frequently noted that his
opinion of his predecessor was just the opposite of the view
Holmes expressed. Poe's C. Auguste Dupin, it is commonly
observed, is a model for Holmes. Urbane, supremely rational,
and idiosyncratic, he is attended by a loyal companion narrator, and often takes on cases the dull police cannot solve.
Given to dispensing axioms about crime, thought, and life
itself, he keeps his methods secret until a final burst of revelation in which everything, especially his own brilliance, be-

comes clear. But beyond these general resemblances between the two detectives, a very particular relation emerges between the last short story in which Dupin appears and the first time Holmes puts in an appearance in short-story form.

Many have been reminded of "The Purloined Letter" when reading "A Scandal in Bohemia," but few have realized the specific nature of that debt. The closer we look, the more curious it gets. For, remarkably, in taking ideas for "A Scandal in Bohemia" from Poe's "The Purloined Letter," Conan Doyle used exactly the same strategy Poe's criminal, Minister D——, used when he pilfered the letter from the queen, leaving the evidence altered, but in plain view.

Poe's famous story, you will recall, turns on a letter that the vile Minister D—— filched from under the nose of the queen and with which he threatens to blackmail her to the king. We are never given the content of the letter, but its nature is easily inferred: it is a compromising note from an admirer. The king surprised her while she was reading it, and having no time to hide the letter, she put it in plain view, address upmost, among the papers on her desk. And indeed the king did not notice it. But Minister D——, who also arrived to visit the royal boudoir on matters of state, did spot the letter, recognized its author's handwriting (and thus its potential value), and switched it for a letter of his own in full view of the queen, without the king's noticing.

The queen, the police, and Dupin know that Minister D—— has the letter, but the problem is laying hands on it. In addition to waylaying him and searching his person in the guise of footpads, Prefect G——'s men have repeatedly ransacked the minister's apartment during his frequent absences, minutely searching for the hidden letter in the cores of chair legs, under table tops, between bookbindings, behind wallpaper, and so forth. Having turned up nothing, the prefect has come to ask Dupin for advice. Dupin suggests the exasperated official make a thorough re-search of the premises. Returning a month later, no more successful than before, Prefect G—— says he would gladly give fifty thousand francs to find the letter. Dupin asks for a check in that amount and, in exchange for it, presents the astonished prefect with the very letter he sought.

Dupin explains he had made his own visit to Minister D——. Wearing dark glasses for an alleged eye condition, he glanced about the apartment as he maintained a "most animated discussion" on a topic calculated to interest and excite the minister. Displayed in a card rack in plain view, a letter caught his eye—a letter in so many particular ways precisely opposite to the one Prefect G—— had described to him that Dupin concluded it must be the item. He left his snuffbox behind, and on making a second visit to retrieve it, Dupin brought a facsimile of the letter he proposed to steal. A hired accomplice created a hubbub in the street by firing an unloaded gun, and as the minister looked down on the disturbance below, Dupin made the switch, leaving the minister ignorant that he was no longer in possession of the queen's letter. Thus the unknowing minister is vulnerable to ruin if he seeks to play that card.

The key to the story is Dupin's method, his identification with the mind of the criminal, a process he explains at length—beginning with the childhood example of a schoolboy who could always guess whether his classmates held an odd or even number of marbles in their hands by deducing from their relative intelligences their likely strategies in the game against him. The minister knew the police would think he would hide the letter very securely; so to outwit them, he left it in plain view. He had taken care to alter its appearance by turning it inside out, changing the seal, and writing his name on it as the addressee. But these reversals only emphasized for Dupin the underlying identity. So it remained only for the detective to fashion an imitation of his own (with a message taunting the minister inscribed inside) and to switch the letters. Dupin has saved the queen from blackmail, delivered a delayed insult to the criminal, and made a tidy profit in the bargain.

"A Scandal in Bohemia" is just like the stolen letter resting in Minister D——'s card rack: it is "The Purloined Letter" turned inside out, with a new name and seal put on it—a bold appropriation, so deft it makes us admire the new owner's ingenuity rather than resent his theft. Our sense of Conan Doyle's art as well as his debt increases as we see the main points of reversal by which the two stories are linked.[6]

Both Poe's queen and Conan Doyle's king are threatened with having illicit liaisons revealed, but the inversions of their situations (and our responses to them) are striking. The most notable reversal, of course, is the change in genders of the aggrieved royalty, a queen in one case, a king in the other, each with a blackmailer of the opposite sex. This inversion is complemented by the reversal of our sympathies in the later tale.

In Poe's story, we know nothing of the queen (both she and the king are purely formal character designations), and we sympathize with the besieged lady's cause from beginning to end. In "A Scandal in Bohemia," our sympathies shift: the more we know of the king, the less we like him. The more we see of Irene Adler, the less we incline to thwart her, especially as we discover she holds the photograph only to protect herself rather than to threaten the king in the way the minister threatened his queen. We may admire the brash aplomb with which Minister D—— tauntingly permits, even encourages, the violent searches of his person and premises. But our sympathies are evoked for Irene Adler, a woman who is the unwilling victim of similar assaults—another significant reversal.

Both Holmes and Dupin use confederates to create a hubbub to aid them at the crucial moment, but in opposite ways. Dupin, by "the identification of the reasoner's intellect with that of his opponent" and a previous inspection of Minister D——'s rooms, knows exactly where the letter is and wants to turn the minister's attention away from it. Conversely, Holmes tricks Irene Adler herself into showing him just where the photo is hidden, knowing that in case of fire "when a woman [as opposed to a man?!] thinks that her house is on fire, her instinct is at once to make for the thing which she values most."

Dupin leaves a substitute letter that the scurrilous black-mailer will find, his capacity to blackmail now eliminated by the wit of the detective. Contrarily, it is Adler who leaves a substitute photograph and letter for the chagrined Holmes to discover, and all threat of blackmail is erased by the promise of the former adventuress, whose virtue is now sealed by her own choice in marriage. This only highlights the final inversion: Holmes fails where Dupin succeeds. Dupin beats the minister at his own game of substituting letters in plain view, whereas Adler, an actress after all, beats Holmes in his game of deduction and disguise—and in doing so, wins her place in his esteem. "And that was how . . . the best plans of Mr. Sherlock Holmes were beaten by a woman's wit."

So the two stories, like the two appearances of the pur-loined letter, are of the same size and type, but with the spe-cifics reversed, turned inside out. Conan Doyle seems to have adapted Dupin's advice and "identified his intellect" with that of his precursor, in order to surpass him by miming his mind and his methods, just as Dupin outwitted the wily minister. ✸

"By the way, Doctor, I shall want your co-operation."
"I shall be delighted."
"You don't mind breaking the law?"
"Not in the least."

For all that he stole, Conan Doyle's story is not the servile imitator of strategies deployed in "The Purloined Letter." "A Scandal in Bohemia" contains its own model for the relation-ship between the two tales, a model of deviation and escape. In just the same way that Holmes shakes free of the influence of the king, Conan Doyle's story steps out from under the shadow of its predecessor—ethically and emotionally, strategically and intellectually.

Poe's story is completely devoid of any moral complexity, but Holmes's switch in allegiance from the king to Irene Adler is at least as significant as the ruse by which he discovers the photograph's location. Dupin avoids the necessity of moral choice because Poe puts him on the right side from the first. Contrarily, Conan Doyle starts Holmes in an immoral position, then makes it clear that his amoral hero has made a moral turn when Holmes delivers his frosty final remarks to the king. In Poe's story, the hero learns nothing; Dupin is unaffected, a catalyst only. But we remember "A Scandal in Bohemia" mainly because in it Holmes was smitten for life with the charms of "*the* woman."

Most importantly, Conan Doyle turns his back on the intellectual principle on which the Poe story rests: Irene Adler hid the photo in just the sort of place that Prefect G——'s men would have first looked and found it. Poe's is a story of brazen exposures and surfaces; Conan Doyle's, a tale of clever disguises and hidden depths.

The logic of disguises I set out earlier in this chapter holds that the disguise actually reveals rather than hides—as Halloween costumes so often do. Rather than concealing, the mask reveals a hidden truth about its wearer. In "A Scandal in Bohemia," this is true not only of characters—Holmes, the would-be groom, or the masked king pretending to be less than a king—but the principle of the revealing disguise touches narrative structures as well. Watson's masquerading as an innocent bystander who in fact lobs a smoke bomb reveals his essential narrative function as the guileless narrator who clouds the case so that Holmes can emerge from the smoke and clarify it with an explanation. And if the detective story form itself is a mask romance sometimes wears, that only highlights the fact that romances—from *Parsifal* to *Love in the Time of Cholera*—are as much about a searching after the truth as they are about gallant men seeking and serving fair ladies.

Though Dupin defends a lady's honor in a scarcely

disguised romance, the logic by which his detection proceeds is a play of surface and exposure—a denial of depth, hiddenness, and disguise. The French psychoanalyst Jacques Lacan, drawn by the surface qualities of this story, analyzes it along lines that combine Freud with suggestions from the early structural linguistics of Ferdinand de Saussure, in which a word's position within a contemporaneous system of language determines its meaning (rather than the older view of meanings based on historical etymologies that are often lost or hidden from sight). Though Lacan's argument is far too subtle and oracular to summarize in its entirety, some of the principal ideas can help us appreciate other critical differences between Conan Doyle's story and its precursor.[7]

Lacan makes much of the fact that the purloined letter itself is a "pure" or empty signifier; its unrevealed contents do not matter. The position—the possession—of the letter is all that counts. In a way, of course, he is fudging, because Lacan, like every reader of the story, infers the nature of the letter's contents. Expressions of an illicit amorous and/or political relationship, they are made more interesting by being withheld, hidden. The photograph in "A Scandal in Bohemia" is more explicit and paradoxical: the picture of the couple together, the very proof of her liaison with the king, is used to defend Adler's virtue.

A second Lacanian point is more intriguing. As this empty signifier changes hands, it gives different meanings to those who possess it. Different character functions are occupied by different personages as the letter moves among them. Lacan schematizes it thus:

> Thus three moments, structuring three glances, borne by three subjects, [are] incarnated each time by different characters.
> The first, is a glance that sees nothing: the King [, then] the police.
> The second, a glance which sees that the first sees

nothing and deludes itself as to the secrecy of what it hides: the Queen, then the Minister.

The third sees that the first two glances leave what should be hidden exposed to whoever would seize it: the Minister, and finally Dupin.

So, in the same way the minister steals from the queen the letter the king does not see, Dupin steals from the minister the letter the police do not discover. As the letter changes hands, the roles once filled by the queen and the minister are next filled by the minister and Dupin. The circulation of the letter determines who fills what slot, what role.

By contrast, the photograph in "A Scandal in Bohemia" does not circulate—Holmes does. Instead of a series of seeings and not seeings, Conan Doyle's story turns on a series of pairings and uncouplings, liaisons, if not always marriages, in which roles shift continuously and volatilely. As the story begins, Watson, recently married, rekindles his old companionship with Holmes, even sleeps again at Baker Street during the climactic night. The anticipated pairing of the king and the princess Clotilde makes the king vulnerable to his previous liaison with Irene Adler. Holmes allies himself with the king, whom he honors and obeys for a time, which distances him from Watson, who is ashamed of the part he plays in Holmes's scheme. Adler's marriage to Norton complicates the meaning of her previous liaison with the king (now as much a potential embarrassment to her as to him). Though she is well matched to Holmes in wits, their covert match in the disguised wedding is an instability settled only when Holmes "weds" the picture she has left behind. As Watson notes, Holmes calls the photograph itself "*the* woman," in an idealized marriage, chaste and secure.

In the course of the tale, Holmes has been paired with Watson, the king, Adler, and finally the photo. As soon as he ceases to circulate, change valence, and recombine, all the other couples settle down. Watson no longer sleeps over at

Holmes's digs; Holmes finally refuses the king's hand and the ring he offers; Irene Adler and Norton elope; and the story concludes with Holmes heading for his chambers, alone, bearing the photograph of Irene Adler. Here, too, each character slot or role has been filled by several different personages: potential blackmailer and blackmailed; aggressor and victim; wit and outwitted; lover and beloved. What has circulated and changed the meanings of those he contacts is not an empty signifier that demonstrates what Lacan claims is "the preeminence of the signifier over the subject," but rather a character, a subject who himself changes and recognizes the changes in himself and others.

Lacan concludes his seminar with a maxim now grown famous in critical circles: "the sender . . . receives from the receiver his own message in reverse form. Thus it is that what the 'purloined letter' . . . means is that a letter always arrives at its destination." In short, turning a letter inside out really only reveals its originally unstated unconscious meanings. The same should apply to reversing or "misreading" a story, as Conan Doyle did. The reversed story should reveal features of the original that previously remained unconscious. Until now, I have mainly used Poe's original to show the features of Conan Doyle's later, reversed story more clearly. But certainly "A Scandal in Bohemia" sends a letter back to Poe and throws into relief certain questions about the "unconscious" of the original tale from which it purloined so much.[8]

With Conan Doyle's "A Scandal in Bohemia" in mind, we might well look again at the dubious honor of the French queen, which Dupin so loyally defends (and we could use that to revisit the problematic central role adultery plays in romances from Lancelot and Guinevere, Tristan and Isolde forward). Or Holmes's fascination with a photographic souvenir left for another man could lead us to ask about the peculiar delight the minister might take in reading, possessing another man's private letter to the queen (the signifier, after all, was not pure or empty to him!). And remembering the Holmesian maxim that "it is a capital mistake to theorize before one has data," we might wonder just what the hyperrational Dupin knows as he declares, before the prefect has given him a single detail, "Perhaps the mystery is a little *too* plain. . . . A little *too* self-evident."

Any of these might next take our attention in this coda that is already beginning to wag the chapter. But there is one especially striking way in which Conan Doyle's story illuminates Poe's and shows us (to use Holmes's language) something we previously saw but did not observe. And that is the role of disguise. ❋

> *"Full of these ideas, I prepared myself with a pair of green spectacles."*

The principle that the disguise reveals the inner reality applies to Dupin and the minister as surely as it does to the king and Sherlock Holmes. Disguises are scant in Poe's tale of exposed surfaces, but they are still revealing. In the meeting that turns the tale, Dupin dons dark glasses and the pretense of weak eyes, and the deceitful minister masks his alertness by "yawning, lounging, and dawdling," pretending to be indolent. But in fact, the minister really *is* lazy. Rather than devise a technique of his own to conceal the letter he has pinched, he has simply stolen from the queen herself the principle of hiding it. As she "hid" the letter by leaving it in plain view, so did he.

Dupin's disguise is a pair of dark glasses behind which he glances about and finds the reversed letter, while as a verbal camouflage he "maintained a most animated discussion with the Minister, on a topic which I knew well had never failed to interest and excite him." Dupin then steals the letter after creating a hubbub of distraction. This little subterfuge in disguise reveals what Dupin is actually doing in the story. For he (or should I say Poe) does not acknowledge that the calculating minister simply mimed the queen's panicked move, "exaggerating and extending" the principles by which she operated just as the police exaggerated and extended the principles of their search.

Behind his dark glasses, Dupin does not let us see what he has spied. Instead, stopping the action and addressing the narrator, he holds forth a topic that has "never failed to interest and excite" *us:* ratiocination, the intellectual solution of crimes. He delivers a lecture complete with discourses and analogies involving games of odd and even, the difficulty of finding larger rather than smaller words on maps and shop signs, discovering another's thoughts by imitating his facial expression, the relative reasoning powers of poets and mathematicians, the relation of moral to intellectual principles, the resemblance of algebra to pagan fables, and the purity of abstract reason—all but the first two of which are quite irrelevant to his spotting what the minister is up to. Dupin and Poe distract us with a hubbub of ratiocination while simply pilfering the queen's desperate, intuitive strategy for hiding the letter, and the minister's strategy for stealing it—all spelled out nicely in the account of the original crime given by Prefect G——.[9]

Dupin did indeed identify with the mind of his opponent, but with weak eyes he failed to see (or with shifty eyes, failed to mention) the simplicity of what he had done. His talk of reason is as much a distraction as the shot his accomplice fired outside the minister's window. If we take it seriously, we are like the duped minister who is left with Dupin's facsimile letter in the end, mistakenly believing he is in possession of the genuine article.

In a word, there is much less reasoning here than meets the eye—a frequent characteristic of the Sherlock Holmes stories as well. We appreciate the show of intellection, as in another tale Holmes appreciated the elaborate puzzle of the Red-Headed League—and then we realize that some other principle of operation lies beneath the plot. Poe himself has identified with the mind of the reader, and given us pleasure by seeming to reveal thought's subtlest secrets, leaving for us to discover, if we will, the simple repetitions that ground one of his most effective tales. "Perhaps the mystery is a little *too* plain. . . . A little *too* self-evident."

Dupin was not taken in by his own rhetoric, or tempted to mime the minister's move. Where, in the end, did the detective hide the letter when he got his hands on it? Presented with the check for fifty thousand francs, he turned and, "unlocking an *escritoir,* took thence a letter and gave it to the Prefect." Was he playing odd and even with his opponent?—or simply proving that for the master detective, as for Irene Adler, the old hiding places are the best after all?

PSYCHOLOGIZING THE TEXT OF A *Study in Scarlet*: REPRESSION AND THE TEXTUAL UNCONSCIOUS

*The reader may set me down as a hopeless busybody, when
I confess how much this man stimulated my curiosity. . . .
I eagerly hailed the little mystery which hung around my
companion, and spent much of my time in endeavoring to
unravel it.*

How utterly peculiar Sherlock Holmes must have seemed to
those unprepared readers who first paged through *A Study in
Scarlet,* the novel in which he made his debut. All the traits that
are now familiar, even endearing, were to his first readers
alternately intriguing and appalling—and eminently mysterious. Since the beginning, Holmes fans have, like Watson,
been "endeavoring to unravel" the mystery that surrounds the
detective; and given the man's bizarre combination of eccentricity and brilliance, it is no surprise psychoanalysis has
tempted many readers. Writing *The Seven-Percent Solution,* Nicholas Meyer gave fullest vent to that impulse and imagined
Freud himself analyzing Holmes in the course of curing him
of his cocaine addiction. Others—insightful fans or bemused
academics—have sought to ground Holmes's psychology in

Conan Doyle's. But the urge to put the detective (or the author) on the couch sidesteps the fact that Holmes, after all, is a
literary character, and we meet him in a literary text.

Does this mean we should refrain from psychological
analysis? Not in the least. But it does suggest an eccentric
psychologizing, one centered in the text rather than the hero.
What I want to propose here is the notion that there is a
psychological economy for whole texts as well as for individual
people, for fictions as well as for the characters that inhabit
them. The task will be to posit, discover, and probe the psyche
of text itself. And the text of *A Study in Scarlet* gives us plenty to
look at.

Where to begin? With narratives as with the human
psyche, it is the inconsistent moment, the false gesture—the
slip—that so often gives us the clue that leads to the heart of
the matter, the obscured motivation, the repressed feeling.
That is certainly true here. *A Study in Scarlet* establishes much
that we think most characteristic of the Holmes canon. But it is
also deeply flawed, inconsistent. This novel's most conscious
and memorable literary strategies are dramatically undercut by
other elements of the text itself, and these flaws point to the
existence of a textual unconscious. Appropriately enough, the
telling fault in the tale's conscious "personality" is one of its
most frequently noticed and least understood features.

Though there are more complex and elegant ways of
saying it, the most obvious distinction between consciousness
and the unconscious is quite fundamental. Consciousness
contains what we know and includes what we remember and
who we think we are. By definition, the unconscious consists of
psychological elements we are not aware of (can't remember
or never consciously knew), and, in some cases, are glad to
forget—even though these forgotten and unknown things affect us in ways we do not recognize.

This distinction well describes the two halves of *A Study in
Scarlet,* for it is a book profoundly divided—not only between
what Holmes knows and what he doesn't, but divided between
things we find characteristically Sherlockian and love remem-

bering, and other things we find incongruous and would be glad to forget Conan Doyle ever wrote. Among the elements we remember and relish: the introduction of Watson, the wounded veteran, to Holmes, the eccentric who beats corpses to see how long after death bruises may be produced; the establishment of their residence at 221-B; the assembling of the Baker Street Irregulars; Watson's (dismissed!) suspicion that Holmes might be a drug addict. We witness the detective's skill in the "science of deduction," as he reads Watson's recent history from his appearance ("You have been in Afghanistan, I perceive") and then deduces (from the tangled skein of cart tracks and footsteps, from the word written in blood on the wall and the wedding ring that tumbles to the floor) the height, age, smoking habits, complexion, and probable employment of the murderer in this case, which he has been asked to help solve by the unfailingly failing detectives Gregson and Lestrade.

This last item—Holmes's much touted ability to reason backward to the sources of things—constitutes his most distinguishing mark. It is what everyone knows about Holmes, what we all remember, what is most "elementary" about our enjoyment. His wit in the science of deduction is amplified by his witty repartee, the urbane and controlled flow of language that we reread with relish. And of course what we all prize about the *telling* of these adventures is Watson's narration, this story "Being a Reprint from the Reminiscences of John H. Watson, M.D., Late of the Army Medical Department." The good doctor runs along the trail Holmes pursues just slowly enough for us to keep up and pass occasionally, his admiration and astonishment a chorus to our own.

So it is remarkable that in this novel that first introduced Holmes and Watson to the reading public, *the two features of the canon that we most value and consider most characteristic—Watson's narration and Holmes's reasoning backward to the sources of things— are precisely the deeply flawed, inconsistent elements.* Both are oddly and seriously skewed, disrupted by the novel's textual unconscious in a richly revealing way.

The telling flaw is most evident at the often remarked but little-understood division between the first and second halves of the novel. Turning the page from part 1 to part 2, we encounter a different textual personality. At this point, both consistent narration and analytic reasoning from effect to cause collapse, the genre of story changes, the ethical standings of characters are reversed, and the style of presentation alters dramatically. The differences between parts 1 and 2 are as radical as the differences between the conscious and the unconscious mind—and the book's two parts are related in much the same way as those two aspects of the human personality.

The first jolt we experience is a shift in narrative stance. Part 1 is presented as a reprint from Watson's reminiscences. After introducing us to Holmes, Watson narrates the investigation of the London crimes from the moment they first come to his and Holmes's attention up to the arrest of the perpetrator. Part 2 begins with an account of the events, enacted in America years before, that led to the crimes Holmes has now solved. We see this history through a powerful, omniscient, and distinctly un-Watsonian eye. (So different is the narration here that Jack Tracy's *Encyclopaedia Sherlockiana* slyly attributes authorship of part 2 to Conan Doyle rather than Watson.) Only in the last dozen pages of part 2 does the narrative shift again to "A Continuation of the Reminiscences of John Watson, M.D.," to complete the frame tale begun in part 1.

The crucial point about this narrative shift is that during the course of the story the information in the American saga, which is *the emotional foundation of the novel, never reaches the principals, Watson and Holmes.* The events that unfold on the great blank plains of the American West entirely motivate the action in London. Yet Holmes, who prides himself on getting to the sources of things, is never aware of anything earlier than the killer's shadowing in Cleveland the men who will become his victims in London. Holmes and Watson never investigate and never learn of the early events and emotions that lie at the roots of all the novel's actions.

So, the American saga relates to the London frame narrative as the unconscious relates to the conscious mind. It motivates action and shapes character but remains unknown to the actor, buried in the remote past. It compensates for the excesses in the conscious attitudes of the frame narrative. And it subverts the book's professed conscious purpose and intent. This narrative and psychological split alerts us to other corresponding splits in *A Study in Scarlet*—splits in voice, splits in characterization, splits in the codes of value that define the meanings of actions, and splits in the psyches of individual characters themselves.

To appreciate these, we need to review the facts of the case as the novel presents them—first the introduction of Holmes and the London crimes he solves, and then their origins in the American West. This will give us a chance to revisit some of Conan Doyle's best moments—and some of his worst—allowing us to sense the dynamics that knit the narrative present to its unremembered past. Here, then, are the principal events and key details of the narrative that launched Sherlock Holmes into the public's awareness and won him an unchallenged place in our imaginations. ❋

"There is no branch of detective science which is so important and so much neglected as the art of tracing footsteps."

The tale begins as Watson, wounded and returned from Afghanistan, searches for an amiable and inexpensive living situation, toward which end an old acquaintance introduces him to Holmes. They meet in the chemical laboratory of the same hospital in which Watson's friend has seen Holmes in the dissecting room, beating the corpses to determine how long after death bruises may be produced. When Watson meets him, Holmes is flush with the excitement of devising a positive test for bloodstains, a test for want of which many criminals have escaped the net of justice. Holmes turns from his discovery to interview his potential flat-mate. Comparing a list of personal quirks, each finds the other unobjectionable, and they agree to share the rooms at 221-B Baker Street.

There, Watson is puzzled by Holmes's steady and diverse stream of visitors: in what business might they be clients? Equally perplexing are the strengths and deficiencies of Holmes's knowledge. His study in geology, for example, includes differentiating colors of mud from various parts of London, but he claims surprise and indifference to the notion that the earth revolves about the sun. Such knowledge is of no use to him. At breakfast one morning, Watson peruses a magazine article claiming extraordinary powers for the science of deduction. He pronounces it "ineffable twaddle," but Holmes claims the honor of authorship, explaining how by that very science he had deduced Watson had been in Afghanistan. More formal work at detection is not far away as Holmes receives Inspector Tobias Gregson's request to examine the scene of a recent murder. Holmes invites Watson along, and we follow in his footsteps.

Footprints and cab wheel tracks are Holmes's concern as he and Watson alight from their hansom a hundred yards from their destination and use the rest of the approach to examine the earth made soft by last night's rain. Once inside the house, Holmes and Watson are conducted by Inspector Gregson and his colleague Lestrade to the room of the crime and to the corpse, the latter distinguished by an expression of horror on his apelike visage, the former by bloodstains on the floor (odd, since the victim was not wounded) and the single word "RACHE" scrawled on the wall in blood. "Rache," Holmes explains, is not an incomplete spelling of Rachel, as the Yard surmised, but German for "revenge," a false clue planted to point to German socialist perpetrators and political motives, rather than the personal ones Holmes suspects.

Matching the false clue is a true one. When the body is lifted, a woman's wedding band falls off of the stretcher and into the plot, leading Gregson to conclude a woman had been there, but turning Holmes to other private speculations. A monogram and a letter in the corpse's pocket suggest he is Enoch Drebber, late of Cleveland, Ohio, while a second letter and an inscription on the flyleaf of a copy of the *Decameron* point to his association with one Joseph Stangerson. A glance at the corpse's distorted face and a sniff at his lips tell Holmes the murder was a poisoning. Reflecting for a moment on other clues offered him, Holmes proposes a description of the perpetrator, down to his height, age, florid complexion, long fingernails, and preference for Trichinopoly cigars. With Watson, he departs for the house of the constable who found the body, from whom he discovers that a "drunk sort of man" had turned up outside the abandoned house during the constable's investigation—a man whose height and flushed countenance matched the description Holmes had just proposed.

Back at 221-B, Watson confides to the reader that the "distorted, baboon-like countenance of the murdered man" had given him such disquiet that he could not feel "anything but gratitude for him who had removed its owner from the world." Holmes, meanwhile, reveals a more practical, less emotional, turn of mind. He has placed an advertisement in Watson's name offering to return to its rightful owner the wedding band found in the neighborhood where the crime occurred; and when an apparently elderly woman appears to claim it, Holmes gives her a facsimile and attempts to follow her to her destination, only to be given the slip, leaving him for the moment without a direction.

Directions are suggested the next day by Tobias Gregson, who arrives at Baker Street to announce he has apprehended the criminal in the person of Arthur Charpentier, son of the former landlady to Drebber and Stangerson. Though the trail turns out to be a false one, it leads us to Mrs. Charpentier and her account of Drebber's lewd advances to the serving girls, his eviction from the house, his drunken return and proposition to her daughter on the night of the crime, an insult avenged by a drubbing at the hands of the now-incarcerated Arthur.

Though the information proves useful to limn in Drebber's unsavory character, Gregson's theory is deflated by the arrival of Lestrade, who had been following his own false trail to the new residence of his chief suspect, Joseph Stangerson, only to find him knifed, thus compounding the killing, but exculpating the two most obvious suspects, the one jailed while the other was killed. Lestrade does, however, bring from Stangerson's room a box containing two small gray pills, which Holmes believes to be of the same poison that killed Drebber. As proof, Holmes gamely administers portions to a suffering terrier his landlady wants to put out of its pain. The first pill is evidently a placebo, producing no effect; but the second does the work with dispatch. As the four ponder the defunct canine, a cabman, summoned by one of the Baker Street Irregulars, arrives to take Holmes on a heretofore unannounced trip. As the cabby leans forward to help the detective strap his suitcase, Holmes slips the handcuffs on him. After subduing this strong and resisting prisoner, whose lunge for the window could intend either suicide or escape, Holmes announces that he has apprehended one Jefferson Hope, the culprit in this affair, and offers to answer any questions the Scotland Yard detectives (not to mention Watson and the reader) may have.

With the guilty party apprehended, we wait to discover how the crimes came to be and to hear the chain of reasoning by which Holmes deduced the killer's identity and brought about his appearance at the flat. It is history we get—but not from the world's only consulting detective nor from the man he snared.

Here the novel's second section begins—with a sharp break in the narrative frame. A solemn, omniscient voice describes a scene that occurred on the Great Alkali Plains of the American West some forty-odd years before. "An observer, . . . had there been anything but buzzards to see it," would have witnessed a pathetic sight: an exhausted man and a little girl, survivors of an ill-fated western migration, who face their imminent deaths and discuss in wretched prose the consolation of joining their loved ones in heaven. John Ferrier and little Lucy fall asleep from exhaustion only to be discovered in each other's arms by Brother Stangerson, one of the "ten thousand" Mormons making their way west.[1] On Brigham Young's stern condition that they subscribe to Mormon beliefs, the two waifs join their fates to those of the Latter-Day Saints and make for Utah, where, over a period of a dozen years, they prosper. John Ferrier adopts Lucy as his daughter and becomes, through acumen and hard work, one of the twelve wealthiest men in Salt Lake City, even as his charge blooms through adolescence to become "the flower of Utah." Ferrier's own abhorrence of polygamous marriage keeps him celibate and governs Lucy's prospects as well. She shall not become a "heifer" in the harem of a Mormon patriarch.

While out riding one day, Lucy becomes entangled (appropriately enough) in a herd of cattle and is rescued by Jefferson Hope, whose name betokens his American character and amorous aspirations. Smitten by love, it is Lucy that Hope hopes for. He abandons prospecting for silver and seeks to improve his prospects for marriage, becoming a close friend of the family, worthy to pluck its bloom, the flower of Utah. After having secured Ferrier's blessing, Hope departs to arrange his affairs, promising to return in two months to claim his bride.

At the end of one month, Brigham Young himself arrives at the estate to question Ferrier's loyalty to the church and its tenets, citing his celibacy and rumors that Lucy is betrothed to a "Gentile." Young's mandate is clear and stark: Lucy shall marry a polygamous Mormon. She may in the next month choose either Enoch Drebber or Joseph Stangerson to wed. When the two suitors arrive to vie for her hand, Ferrier drives them from the property, but his power is temporary and small against the Mormon band. Even his house is not secure against mysterious nocturnal visitors who, Conan Doyle would have us believe, actually enter undetected every single night for a month and mark on floor, walls, or ceiling the decreasing number of days that remain for Lucy to make her choice. Her fate is literally in the handwriting on the wall.

The besieged two repose their hope in Hope, who manages to return on the last day to spirit them out of their home and beyond the reach of the Mormons. The second day on the trail, Hope leaves their encampment once in search of food and returns only to find Ferrier dead and crudely buried, and Lucy gone—abducted. Following the trail back to the periphery of Salt Lake City, he finds that it was Stangerson who killed Lucy's adopted father, while Drebber has now taken her as his (yes) eighth wife. Naturally, under these circumstances, the flower of Utah withers and dies within the month. Into the wake strides Jefferson Hope, who presses his lips to her cold forehead and takes the wedding ring from her finger, vowing "she shall not be buried in that." He makes a few attempts on the lives of Stangerson and Drebber—bullets shot through windows, boulders pushed off cliffs—but they are unsuccessful. Daring but "above all things practical," Hope plots a revenge that begins with a return to his Nevada mines for a year to "amass money enough to allow him to pursue his object without privation."

"A combination of circumstances" keeps him at the mines for five years, not one. Returning to Salt Lake City, he finds there has been a schism between the church's young and old. Drebber and Stangerson, among other youth, have been pronounced Gentiles and thus, like himself, exiles from the land. Still bent on revenge, he tracks them for years and almost catches them in Cleveland, where, however, they have the luck to glimpse him just as he sees them. There he is taken into custody by the local authorities for harassment, and the unholy pair flee to Europe, where Hope later follows their trail from city to city, finally arriving in London.

Back in London, the narrative departs from this omniscient account, which no one but the reader has heard, and returns to "Dr. Watson's journal, to which we *[we?]* are already under such obligations." You will recall that Holmes has just arrested the cabbie, Jefferson Hope. Holmes, Watson, Lestrade, and Gregson use Hope's own cab to take their captive from Baker Street to jail, where he makes two revelations. First, he asks Watson to feel the palpitations in his chest, which the doctor correctly concludes indicate an aortic aneurism. Second—precisely because he believes his bursting heart may not let him live to stand trial—he wishes to give his own "account of the business [so he will not] be remembered as a common cut-throat."

It is important to notice that the account Hope gives to the London investigators includes virtually nothing of what the reader has learned in the Mormon melodrama. That entire sequence of the narrative is virtually dismissed. Here is all Holmes and his companions hear of it:

> It don't much matter to you why I hated these men. . . ; it's enough that they were guilty of the death of two human beings—a father and a daughter—and that they had, therefore, forfeited their own lives. . . . [Since] it was impossible for me to secure a conviction against them in any court . . . I determined that I should be judge, jury, and executioner all rolled into one. You'd have done the same, if you have any manhood in you, if you had been in my place.
>
> That girl I spoke of was to have married me twenty years ago. She was forced into marrying that same Drebber, and broke her heart over it. I took the marriage ring from her dead finger, and I vowed that his dying eyes should rest upon that very ring, and that his last thoughts should be of the crime for which he was punished. . . . If I die tomorrow, as is likely enough, I die knowing that my work in this world is done, and well done.

A sketchy and barren account, to be sure. In fact, Hope spends almost as many lines describing how he came to get a job as a cabman in London as he does outlining the causes for his revenge.

As a cabby, he explains, he dogged the paths of the criminal pair right up to their projected departure from England. After Drebber left the station (and, in effect, renewed his crime as a sexual imposer by propositioning his landlady's daughter), it was Hope's cab he selected to flee the girl's angry brother. In that cab, Hope took Drebber to the abandoned house where he exacted his revenge, accompanied by the mysteriously visible spirits of John Ferrier and Lucy. First showing his victim the wedding ring he took from Lucy's finger, Hope made a peculiar proposition—that Drebber choose between two pills Hope had made up when he worked in a medical laboratory. Hope himself would take the other pill. One was harmless; the other deadly poison. "Let the high God judge between us. Choose and eat. . . . Let us see if there is justice upon the earth, or if we are ruled by chance." So excited that the blood ran from his nose, Hope shared the pills with Drebber and proved to himself at least the unerring grasp of the hand of justice. Drebber died; Hope lived. With his own hand he wrote "Rache"—revenge—on the wall, indeed intending it as a false clue and not seeing its personal appropriateness. Leaving the scene, he inadvertently dropped the ring for which he later returned to search, miming drunkenness to escape the constable's suspicion. It was a confederate he later sent to respond to Holmes's advertisement, retrieve the ring, and give Holmes the slip.

Hope then tells how he sought out Stangerson and made him the same offer of the choice of pills. But Stangerson fought back, and Hope had to stab him "in self-defence," piously convinced "It would have been the same in any case, for Providence would never have allowed his guilty hand to pick out anything but the poison." Ethically, "you may consider me to be a murderer, but I hold that I am just as much an officer of justice as you are." This confession delivered, Hope dies that night of his aneurism and is found the next day on the floor of his cell with a "placid smile upon his face . . . [sign of] a useful life, and work well done."

Back at Baker Street once again, Holmes explains his maneuvers, chief among them his counting the cabby into the plot rather than assuming the cab tracks were mere evidence of transportation provided; his telegraphing Cleveland to ask of the marital circumstances of Drebber, thus finding the name of Hope, an "old rival in love" arrested for harassing him; and his deduction of the florid face of the killer from the nose blood on the floor of the murder room. Having determined the name and occupation of the murderer, Holmes sent out his Irregulars in search of a cabby named Jefferson Hope, who not being known in this city would have no reason to change his name. Once Hope was located, Holmes summoned his cab for an ostensible journey. When the cabman arrived, Holmes cuffed him, and the rest, as we say, is history.

❋

> *"In fact, I have written a little monograph upon the subject. . . . Now let me endeavor to show you the different steps in my reasoning."*

Even in summary form, it is clear that two very different types of tales interact to form this one short novel. To show just how thoroughly they relate as the unconscious relates to conscious mind, we need the theory of personality types developed by Carl Jung and his followers. Jung, of course, is chiefly remembered for his theories about the archetypes of the collective unconscious. There is certainly plenty of archetypal material in this novel, and we will touch upon its most remarkable features later. But equally valuable to psychology—and, I contend, to literature—is Jung's comprehensive theory of psychological types. To be able to analyze the personality of the novel, we need first to understand how Jung's theory operates on its home ground, the human personality.

Briefly, the theory goes like this. There are four ways in which an individual can orient him- or herself toward the world—through thinking, feeling, sensation, or intuition. Each of us uses all these functions to a greater or lesser degree. In his briefest formulation of the different functions, Jung says that *"sensation* (i.e., sense perception) tells you that something exists; *thinking* tells you what it is; *feeling* tells you whether it is agreeable or not; and *intuition* tells you whence it comes and where it is going."[2] Though all four functions are present in everyone, each individual typically utilizes one of them more consistently (and more reliably) than the others—to such a degree that it comes to form the style of one's personality and relation with the world. This predominance establishes the person as a thinking type, a feeling or sensation type, or an intuitive. The thinking type excels at ordering experience conceptually, analyzes and categorizes with ease. Flow charts and diagrams, outlines and logical schemas come naturally to thinking types, producing logical hierarchies that (they would claim) reflect the way the world is ordered. They make good planners, engineers, and lawyers, are better at managing systems than relating to other people, and often express little emotion.

The feeling type also orders experience hierarchically, but on quite a different basis. Feelings of ethical rightness or agreeability are paramount (not that those two always coincide), and all logical argument is quite secondary to a clear moral imperative. Feeling types prefer people-centered jobs: health care, pastoral work, journalism, and sales. Tenacity, dedication, and loyalty mark their characters.

The sensation type, like the intuitive (and unlike the thinking and feeling types), experiences life non-hierarchically. With a natural eye for details, large and small, important and seemingly insignificant, and lacking a penchant to prioritize, the sensate type will notice facts that elude others. The visual artist, the designer, the accountant, the warehouse supervisor, not to mention the collector, the bibliographer, the massage therapist, and the dancer are likely to be dominant in sensation.

The intuitive type experiences the world very differently. Though the data may seem aimed in a particular direction or just inconclusive, the intuitive often has a contrary hunch, a "feeling," an inkling, that despite appearances, or even in the absence of evidence, things are going to turn out in a certain way. Not just palm readers and psychics but stockbrokers and theoretical scientists are typically numbered among the intuitives. (Think of Einstein's pronouncement that his theory of relativity "did not come from the rational mind" or of Kekule's discovering the structure of the benzene ring after dreaming of the archetypal snake biting its tail.) And because it can envision what others cannot see, intuition also runs high in the creative arts.

The theory of psychological types is particularly interesting because it not only accounts for divergent personality styles, but for the different psychological forces within a single personality. Those internal dynamics can be illustrated visually.

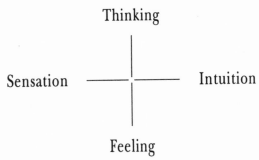

FIG. 2. THE FOUR PSYCHOLOGICAL FUNCTIONS

The four functions are paired in two oppositions: thinking and feeling on one axis, sensation and intuition on the other. Whichever function is dominant in a given personality, its opposite on that axis is inferior—the least used, and the least developed. The other two functions may be more or less available to consciousness. Above, I have given the schema for the thinking type. For the thinker, intuition and sensation are also more or less available, though secondary, and feeling is most distant from consciousness, most unconscious, most difficult to utilize in a skillful and differentiated way. Thus the thinking type will most often have trouble with feeling. Simple rotation of the diagram will produce the pattern for the other types. For the intuitive type, intuition is uppermost, feeling and thinking may be more or less available, and sensation—

dealing with the concrete world of physical facts—will often be crude and bumbling at best.

Typically, the inferior function is split off and lives a kind of crude, second-rate, often unacknowledged life of its own in our psyches, though it may burst onto the conscious scene in times of crisis. It is associated with the shadow, the name Jung gave to the counterpersonality that each of us harbors—the part of ourselves that we deny, neglect, even despise. Under-developed, clumsy, or inappropriate in its expression, the inferior function thus has the potential to disrupt or undermine our conscious lives. The feeling of the thinking type will tend to be crude and undifferentiated. It can erupt in moments of bathos, or even a lifetime of misery: consider the maudlin feeling that brings ruin to the professor in *The Blue Angel*. In a similar way, the feeling type's thinking will tend to force experience onto the Procrustean bed of a few simple, doctrinaire ideas—Ezra Pound. Or the down-to-earth, practical sensation type may find himself taken over by cultish, theosophical mysticism—Conan Doyle himself attending séances. And the sensation function of the intuitive is usually equally inept: consider the common inability of intuitives and visionaries to manage the concrete details of daily life (Karl Marx, unable to feed his family) or their tendency to give themselves over to physical excesses in, say, food, sex, or pain. ❋

"Yes; I have a turn for both observation and deduction . . . . [and] I have a kind of intuition."

Sherlock Holmes is, of course, a classic thinking type, but his lateral functions, sensation and intuition, are well developed too. In fact one of his chief talents is to suspend thinking's tendency toward hierarchy long enough so it does not inhibit his collecting apparently meaningless data. And he relies more than he might admit on intuition—guesswork, as detractors might call it. (Watson's tan and military wound could as logically have been acquired in South Africa as in Afghanistan, for example.) But it is thinking that characterizes his style. The account of "logical inferences" with which he closes each tale gives us such delight that we return to the stories again and again.

With an extravagance that makes us both smile and grimace as we read, the demented inferiority of Holmes's feeling function completes the psychological pattern of the thinking type. In this tale, he beats corpses to see how far after death bruises may be produced; he determines that a pair of pills are placebo and poison by administering them to his landlady's ailing dog, who expires in a "convulsive shiver" at Holmes's feet as he blithely expounds his evolving theory. Here, as elsewhere, it is not moral indignation that sets him on the trail of crime, but intellectual curiosity. The irrational and supernatural are equally unremarked. He has no interest in the eerie shades of Lucy and Ferrier who guided Hope to the scene of the murder nor in the theological ground of Hope's pharmaceutical roulette. He yawns during Gregson's description of the passionate domestic row that drove Drebber from the Charpentier household. Nor is sexuality of interest to Holmes. He neither knows nor wants to know about the romantic stirrings that drew Hope and Lucy to one another, nor about Lucy's abduction and sexual subjugation at the hands of the Mormons.[3] Later, in "A Scandal in Bohemia," he will epitomize this attitude in his famous pronouncement that the passions, love in particular, are like "grit in a sensitive instrument." It is a key element of his bizarre charm that this detective is so defective in feeling. ✳

"A study in scarlet, eh? Why shouldn't we use a little art jargon?"

As I promised, interesting as we may find the personality of Sherlock Holmes, it is not just his psychology but the psyche of the text that is in question here. The split between the two parts of *A Study in Scarlet* is well embodied in the two nouns of its title, cerebral and passionate. In part 1, we have the conscious personality of the text: urbane, rational, and distinctly lacking in feeling. Not just Holmes, but the other detectives try to proceed on a rational basis; they find the crimes interesting rather than being moved by their horror. The second half of the novel is precisely the opposite. Here is where feeling lives—in the story of which the Londoners are unconscious. The values of the novel's two halves are the reverse of one another. The villain of part 1 is the hero of the Mormon melodrama, and all the feeling that Holmes does not display finds expression in Jefferson Hope. The opposite of Holmesian detachment, Hope is first smitten with love and later possessed by revenge—a Fate, a nemesis driven by moral righteousness. His methods are not elegant and rational but determined and dogged. Sixty recorded adventures punctuate Holmes's life with interest; one crime dominates Hope's life with passion.

Every aspect of the text is permeated by this difference: plot, style, other characters. Balancing the urbane and cerebral values of part 1, which are qualified only occasionally by a shudder of feeling from Watson, the novel's second half is dominated by crude, mawkish feeling—*feeling as Holmes himself would characterize it and suppress it*—the stuff of the most purple (or scarlet) melodrama. The two waifs rescued in the parched desert by a band of traveling Mormons, the blossoming of the flower of Utah and her rescue by Hope on horseback, Lucy cast into the harem of the elder's son and dying of a broken heart, and Jefferson Hope's unswerving vow of revenge—all these are the most hackneyed elements of romance, literary boilerplate.[4] The American saga is filled with feeling that is rooted in certainties of faith. Lucy's childlike piety, Ferrier's resistance to the Mormon "perversions," Jefferson Hope's conviction that his vengeance is God's justice—all this contrasts starkly to Holmes's skeptical and amoral empiricism.[5] The interpolated narrative is the moral center of the tale, and its center of feeling. The entire chain of events springs from it.

But, as we have seen, Holmes never hears this passion-drenched account of motivation.[6]

As readers, we may consider Holmes lucky in this regard, for not only are the emotionally charged events themselves bathetic, but the restrained and witty prose style that we appreciate in the detective story of part 1 is replaced in part 2 by the style of sentimental romance, and the urbane musings of the Londoners are supplanted by crude American dialogue. Here is a fair taste.

> "Then mother's a deader too," cried the little girl, dropping her face in her pinafore and sobbing bitterly. . . .
> "I guess that's about the size of it."

It is not just the dialogue. Conan Doyle's narrative prose here also takes frequent plunges into the saccharine spring of third-rate romance:

> On such occasions, Lucy was silent, but her blushing cheek and her bright happy eyes showed only too clearly that her young heart was no longer her own.

The bathetic prose pervading the American sentimental romance is the stylistic shadow side of the more polished language featured in the tale of ratiocination that Watson and Holmes inhabit.

Differences in style reinforce other significant splits between the novel's consciousness and its unconscious. Thinking is valued in the frame tale, and feeling is the central value of Mormon melodrama. Holmes seeks to effect legal justice in the narrative present, while Hope sees himself as the agent of divine justice, righting a wrong done in the remote past. Scientific investigation is the guiding model in the London narrative, while moral imperatives and the pieties of faith drive the American heroes. If we diagram these oppositions, putting the textual consciousness above the horizontal line and its uncon-

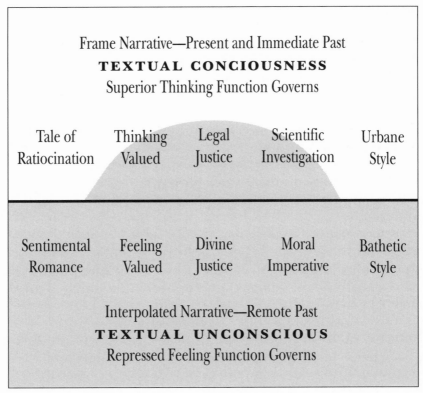

Frame Narrative—Present and Immediate Past

TEXTUAL CONCIOUSNESS

Superior Thinking Function Governs

| Tale of Ratiocination | Thinking Valued | Legal Justice | Scientific Investigation | Urbane Style |

| Sentimental Romance | Feeling Valued | Divine Justice | Moral Imperative | Bathetic Style |

Interpolated Narrative—Remote Past

TEXTUAL UNCONSCIOUS

Repressed Feeling Function Governs

FIG. 3. SUBVERSION OF CONSCIOUS TEXTUAL VALUES
BY THE TEXTUAL UNCONSCIOUS

scious below, a dynamic interaction between the two realms can be illustrated, showing how the qualities of the interpolated events intrude upon the frame narrative itself. The shaded area rising from the bottom of the diagram to the top indicates the degrees to which values from the textual unconscious turn up in the frame narrative and impinge upon its conscious attitudes, just as happens in the human psyche. Centrally, the cause of legal justice is entirely subverted by the simple narrative event of Jefferson Hope's dying when and as he does. The law does not exact its price for the crime, and Hope's serene death from an overfull heart reads as an escape from earthly law rather than as penance or punishment. The code of the textual unconscious simply overturns and replaces the conscious aims of the frame narrative, which are to prevent further murders and to bring the criminal to justice and punish his crime.[7]

As the diagram indicates, the values of the American saga also compromise other conscious attitudes in the story of Holmes and Watson, though in lesser degrees. In general, thinking is still the dominant value of the frame narrative as it draws to a close, but the moral feeling of the Mormon melodrama turns up in the judgment of Dr. Watson. He, alone among the Londoners, dallies with the code of faith long enough to surmise that Hope's death had summoned him "before a tribunal where strict justice would be meted out to him," seemingly persuaded by Hope's peaceful visage that heavenly justice will favor Hope. Watson's charitable reading of that dying face is paired with his earlier reaction to the dead Drebber's appearance, his rush of "gratitude for him who had removed [the] owner . . .[of] the distorted, baboon-like countenance of the murdered man . . . from the world." His judgments are based in immediately intelligible feelings. While the scientifically inclined Holmes was scanning the face of the murdered man for traces of convulsions and sniffing his lips for the odor of poison, Watson saw in the dead man's features the outward signs of an evil soul. His reading Hope's and Drebber's faces as moral icons brings the feeling values of the Mormon melodrama into the main narrative wholesale, without, however, knowing the sequence of events that gave rise to them. Via Watson, feelings from the remote past now appear without apparent cause in the consciousness of the frame narrative, like the influences of the unconscious mind on consciousness.[8]

The sentimental romance stays almost entirely beneath the threshold of the frame tale's awareness; it is scarcely glimpsed in the truncated, erasure-filled, and self-deprecating account Hope gives at the police station. The sentimental, bathetic style, too, is largely abandoned by Hope himself when he at last enters the frame narrative, as if he (or Conan Doyle) recognized that its language was intelligible only when bolstered by the values of the romance plot. As readers, we may be relieved to return to the relative sophistication of Watson's London narrative, but our experience of the events in the West carries weight. Knowing the history behind them, our response to Hope's death and the murders he committed is ambivalent. Our reading is the richer, for we have two distinct satisfactions, appreciating Holmes's detective work (which in a sense comes to nothing) and enjoying Jefferson Hope's revenge (purified by righteous motive and sweet death).

By contrast, Holmes knows—and feels—nothing of that history. He solves the mechanics of the crime, but does not understand it, and thus achieves a very narrow, if intense, form of consciousness. Even solving the crimes, Holmes does nothing to prevent or rectify them. He has no effect on the actions that spring from the American plains. His function is only to know, to reveal who did it, and how. Of the unconscious, he still knows nothing. But it leaves its mark. ❦

Both slept the same deep and dreamless slumber.

Something else important is going on here, something more universal and archetypal. As the events of Utah move out of their remoteness in time and place toward eruption onto the London scene, they form a significant parallel to the universal processes by which the unconscious moves toward consciousness. All schools of depth psychology agree that mental life begins in undifferentiated totality and then proceeds toward consciousness by making distinctions. An infant does not distinguish between sleeping and waking, fantasy and reality, self and other. All is one in the oceanic totality, the original fullness.[9] The first sense of separation comes from threat of privation, which would be death for the helpless infant. The parent is ambiguous, alternately benign as provider and malign as withholder of food, warmth, and affection. This gives rise to the distinction between the good parent and the bad parent. For the male child (let us focus on his case here, since *A Study in Scarlet* is male centered), the split attitude continues in the Oedipal triangle, with the father-protector also being the father-depriver who possesses the female prize against the boy's desires.

Within the self, other distinctions emerge, distinctions that define—that create—consciousness. First the body/mind dichotomy; then the differentiation of the personality the child calls his own from the thoughts and feelings he has but rejects as not really his (and often projects onto others)—defining the ego by creating the shadow. From these initial divisions stem all the this/that, me/world distinctions that constitute our psychological environment. At each level, an original unconscious unity is divided by an act of differentiation, a split that casts the individual's conscious personality into sharper relief—and limits it more severely.

A work of art can gain great power by duplicating in a symbolic way the fundamental processes of the human psyche. *The Metamorphoses, Moby-Dick, Frankenstein, The Sound and the Fury,* not to mention *Creature from the Black Lagoon* and *2001: A Space Odyssey*—a work at any level of seriousness or excellence can symbolically incorporate elements of these primary processes, producing not so much a shock of recognition as a subliminal undercurrent of resonance, as it duplicates and offers images of our psychological evolution toward consciousness. And so it is with *A Study in Scarlet,* which embodies in its textual unconscious some of the most primary psychological paradigms, those just outlined.

The blankness of the primary psyche, unlimited and undifferentiated, is well imaged by the vast and indistinct desert that declines from the Sierra Blanco, the scene that opens part 2. We first discover Lucy and John Ferrier, alone on that large, blank landscape, about to lose consciousness, and with it, life itself. They are saved from extinction by the Mormon band, who become their life-sustaining parents, nurturing the two waifs to health and, over the next dozen years, to prosperity.

But as time passes, the patriarchal elders increasingly assume the role of the despotic parent, demanding obedience from the foundling pair.

When Lucy reaches marriageable age and Jefferson Hope is introduced as the hero figure, the Oedipal configuration is clear. The Mormons play out the role of the withholding father who would possess the sexual prize. With their demand that she marry into the Mormon band, they frustrate the desires of Hope, of Lucy herself, and of John Ferrier, the good father, aligned with the wishes of youth against the elders—a classical configuration, from Greece, through Shakespeare, to television's situation comedies. The good father is murdered, the woman debased by the younger representative of the old, malign patriarchal order.

Hope's reaction to his loss has two phases, and the change from one to another is significant. And his initial attempts at revenge are cartoonishly crude—a bullet shot through Stangerson's window, a boulder toppled toward Drebber on horseback. But when these immediate attacks are unsuccessful, he withdraws from Utah for five years—in order to "amass money enough to allow him to pursue his object without privation." This curious withdrawal is a first advance toward conscious planning rather than impulsive immediacy. And with this move toward consciousness comes a proliferation of the splits in the narrative, which is appropriate, since it is from distinctions that consciousness is made.

Splits appear everywhere we look. A schism has fractured the church, setting the youth against the elders, Hope discovers when he returns to Utah: Drebber and Stangerson have become outcasts, "Gentiles" like himself. A further distinction divides these two apostates from each other: Drebber has become wealthy while Stangerson is impoverished—like Hope, who amassed wealth but later lost it in his pursuit of the two men whose crime was a dark and shadowy version of his own desire to possess Lucy. The fugitives also develop contrary moral inclinations: Drebber becomes increasingly sottish and renews his crime as a sexual imposer, while Stangerson assumes the role of his upright guardian. Hope himself splits simple revenge into the possibilities of murder and suicide. Working in a medical laboratory (as Holmes did), he concocts pairs of pills, poison and placebo, which embody for him moral, even metaphysical, distinctions. "Let the high God judge between us. Choose and eat. There is death in one and life in the other. I shall take what you leave. Let us see if there is justice upon the earth, or if we are ruled by chance."

It should come as no surprise, then, that when Jefferson Hope first appears in the textual consciousness of the narrative frame, it is amid more splitting and mirroring. Summoned to Holmes's flat and apprehended there, Hope, who fled the decrees of the Mormon's Sacred Council of Four, finds himself in the hands of four servants of the secular law at Baker Street: Lestrade, Gregson, Holmes, and Watson. This foursome is itself split between pairs of official and unofficial agents of the law. And as Hope's sanctioned impulse meets the resistance of law, the move toward consciousness is complete, and the elements of the unconscious begin to fade into forgetfulness. ❊

"And now . . . we have reached the end of our little mystery."

A Study in Scarlet is the Genesis of the Sherlock Holmes canon. Psychologically considered, the creation myths of all cultures not only present how the things of this world came to be, but symbolize the dawning of consciousness itself. "Let there be light" does not just conjure up physical illumination; it duplicates the act of will that brings forth consciousness, an increasingly sustained awareness born of distinctions and separations: sky from water, land from sea, day from night, man from woman, good from evil, one people from another. This is a common feature of the creation myths that punctuate the great initiatory texts of all our cultures—from the Bible and Ovid to the Upanishads and Vedas.

Putting a novel by Conan Doyle in this august company exceeds mere eccentricity, I realize. Yet, *A Study in Scarlet* is itself an important initiatory text, one that founded a cult whose numbers today are larger than those who undertook the exodus from Egypt millennia ago. Set aside the facts that devoted Holmes fans routinely refer to the canon as the Sacred Writings, and many are proud to call themselves Holmesian Fundamentalists. I only wish to point out that Conan Doyle has followed the ancient template laid down in creation myths. In fashioning this tale that first brought Sherlock Holmes to consciousness, his and our own, Conan Doyle thoroughly mimed—here as nowhere else[10]—the great myths of the psyche, the movement from the unconscious to consciousness, and the dynamics by which consciousness and the unconscious interact. Though some of the strokes he used were crude and primitive, the pattern is powerfully effective.

Psychologizing the text has taken us far beyond the mind of the protagonist, fascinating as that is to unravel. Quite beyond Holmes's militant rationalism and his rigorous suppression of feeling, we find a text profoundly split in its conscious and unconscious attitudes, as these are embodied in the heroes, ethos, actions, even the prose styles of its two parts. It was a mind-set that Conan Doyle would find burdensome in time, but one for which readers have been continuously grateful. *A Study in Scarlet* serves as a founding myth of a subculture that is one of the broadest and most satisfying in English letters, a beginning that could not know its end.

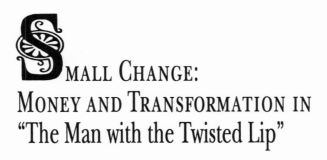

SMALL CHANGE: MONEY AND TRANSFORMATION IN "The Man with the Twisted Lip"

"There is no reason, therefore, to think that money troubles have been weighing upon his mind."

As if to make it clear that he was interested in mystery and not just crime, Conan Doyle wrote a number of Holmes stories in which no illegality is committed. "The Man with the Twisted Lip" is one of the best. The sources of the story's appeal are many—we glimpse the seamy world of opium addiction, see Holmes bow to woman's intuition, and witness a dramatic unmasking. But there is a more fundamental appeal here. The story continues to fascinate because it exercises some of our most enduring fantasies—fantasies not about power or sex or death, but about that least spoken of obsessions: money. ❧

"I'll state the case clearly and concisely to you, Watson, and
maybe you may see a spark where all is dark to me."

The tale begins as Kate Whitney, a friend of Mrs. Watson, interrupts the Watsons' domestic tranquility and frantically asks the doctor to retrieve her husband from a now three-day stay at the Bar of Gold, a notorious opium den he frequents in the seedy neighborhood of Upper Swandam Lane. In the dim confines of the den, Watson finds Isa Whitney, reminds him of his duty to his anxious wife, and convinces him to return home. While in the den, Watson is startled to hear his own name whispered by a thin, dissolute figure who momentarily reveals himself to be Sherlock Holmes and invites Watson to join him on a case. Putting Whitney in a cab and sending a note to Mrs. Watson, he is off on the case with Holmes. Once clear of the den, the detective chuckles that Watson might worry that Holmes had added opium smoking to his cocaine injections. Not so, he reassures us: he too was just looking for someone.

Holmes is glad to quit the Bar of Gold, a dangerous riverside den he has often visited in his investigations, run by a Malaysian Lascar who is his particular enemy. "We should be rich men if we had a thousand pounds for every poor devil who has been done to death in that den. It is the vilest murder-trap on the whole river-side, and I fear Neville St. Clair has entered it never to leave it more." As they head for the country home of Mrs. St. Clair, in Lee, county of Kent, Holmes relates to Watson the facts as he knows them from St. Clair's wife.

Neville St. Clair, a man of temperate habits and plenty of money though no particular profession beyond capital investments, took up residence in Lee some five or six years ago, married three years later, and now has a devoted wife, two children, and a good balance sheet at the bank. The previous Monday, he went to town on what seemed his usual business, promising to buy his son some toy building blocks. Later that same day, his wife by chance received a telegram asking her to retrieve a valuable parcel from the Aberdeen Shipping Company, not far from Upper Swandam Lane. Passing along that street, she was surprised to see her husband, framed in the window above the Bar of Gold opium den, agitated and beckoning, as it seemed to her, only to disappear suddenly from view. She rushed to the door of the den, where she was barred by the strength of the Lascar. By the time she had summoned nearby constables and overcome the protestations of the proprietor and a hideous, wretched beggar who made his home there, it seemed that there was nothing to be found in the room in which her husband had been seen. But the chance discovery of a box of child's building bricks prompted the police to search more carefully, and behind a curtain they found all of Neville St. Clair's clothes, save his coat, later found at low tide, sunk to the river bottom, its pockets loaded with halfpennies and pence.

Having heard the facts, Holmes has developed a theory. He hypothesizes that (for motives never revealed) the beggar hurled St. Clair from the window of his room and had begun to throw his clothes after him, weighing them down with coins he had begged. Unlike the weighted coat, the floating body must have been sucked away down the river.

Holmes inquires into the character of this beggar, one Hugh Boone, the last man to lay eyes on Neville St. Clair. He seems to have lived a quiet and innocent life, and he had achieved something of a reputation in Threadneedle Street, the site of his solicitations (and incidentally the location of the Bank of England). Boone attracted attention to himself with his hideous scarred face, twisted lip, and shocking shock of red hair, as well as with his witty repartee with passersby. He made pretense of selling wax vestas—friction matches—but his income in fact came from the "small rain of charity" given in pity for his disfigurement. Though Holmes has given us a "working hypothesis," he confesses himself still much perplexed by the case, even though Boone is now safely under arrest.

This recollection finished, Holmes and Watson arrive at the St. Clair house, where "the door flew open, and a little blonde woman stood . . . outlined against a flood of light." She

counters Holmes's grim suspicion that St. Clair has been murdered by producing a letter from Neville she received just that
day. The message is clear and reassuring.

> Dearest, do not be frightened. All will come well. There
> is a huge error which it may take some little time to rec-
> tify. Wait in patience.—Neville.

Enclosed with the letter is his signet ring, a powerful reminder
of him, though as Holmes says, it "proves nothing." But in
addition to the letter, there is the force of Mrs. St. Clair's
assertion that "There is so keen a sympathy between us that I
should know if evil came upon him"—and she is certain he
lives. Holmes responds with unusual respect for this woman's
intuition:

> I have seen too much not to know that the impression
> of a woman may be more valuable than the conclusion
> of an analytical reasoner. And in this letter you certainly
> have a very strong piece of evidence to corroborate your
> view.

The very strength of her certainty spurs Holmes to revise his
reading of what she saw at the Bar of Gold: what she took for a
call for help may have been a cry of surprise; when it seemed
he was pulled back from the window, he may have leaped back
instead. Holmes concludes his dialogue with Mrs. St. Clair,
and after a little supper, he and Watson retire to the guest
room of the St. Clair home.

Readers accustomed to Holmes's long and intense
mystery-solving meditations will delight in the style and ex-
tremity of the one at the center of this story. As an exhausted
Watson slips between the sheets, Sherlock Holmes prepares

> for an all-night sitting, . . . collecting pillows from his
> bed, and cushions from the sofa and arm chairs. With

these he constructed a sort of Eastern divan, upon which he perched himself cross-legged, with an ounce of shag tobacco and box of matches laid out in front of him. . . . An old brier pipe between his lips, his eyes fixed vacantly upon the corner of the ceiling, the blue smoke curling up from him, silent, motionless, with the light shining upon his strong-set aquiline features. So he sat as I dropped off to sleep, and so he sat when a sudden ejaculation caused me to wake up, and I found the summer sun shining into the apartment. . . . "Awake, Watson?" he asked.

Having meditated all night, Holmes is now awake to a fresh vision, free of his former delusion.

"I think, Watson, that you are now standing in the presence of one of the most absolute fools in Europe. I deserve to be kicked from here to Charing Cross. But I think I have the key of the affair now."
"And where is it?"
"In the bathroom. . . . I have just been there, and I have taken it out, and I have got it in this Gladstone bag."

With the enigmatic Holmes musing it is "better to learn wisdom late than never to learn it at all," the pair proceed to the prison where Hugh Boone is being held, asleep and unwashed, his face "black as a tinker's." Admitted by the jailer, Holmes slips quietly into the cell and removes from his Gladstone bag a great bath sponge, which he wets and applies to the blackened face of the sleeping Boone. The prisoner awakes in shock and dismay as Holmes wipes the disguise from his face and reveals the beggar to be none other than "Neville St. Clair, of Lee, in the county of Kent." St. Clair is surprised, but also shrewdly defiant: he can be charged with no crime. How, indeed, to charge him with his own murder, when his very presence refutes of the charge? Still, he desperately wants to avoid exposure of his double life, especially to the eyes of his family.

For Holmes and reader alike, St. Clair explains what he hopes the authorities will let pass and no newspaper will recount. Previous to his present occupation, first acting and then newspaper reporting had been his professions, and as a reporter he had drawn upon his thespian skills. Assigned to do an article on begging, he disguised himself as a disfigured beggar and found he could make astoundingly good money at it. Later, short of cash and needing to pay a debt, he returned to begging in disguise and found as a beggar he could make in a single day the two pounds he earned in a week as a reporter.

> It was a long fight between my pride and the money, but the dollars won at last, and I threw up reporting and sat day after day in the corner which I had first chosen, inspiring pity by my ghastly face and filling my pockets with coppers.

Only the Lascar, who rented St. Clair the room above the opium den in which he effected his daily transformation, was privy to his secret—and he guarded it well.

Acknowledging that not just "any beggar in the streets of London could earn seven hundred pounds a year," he found in his piteous and impenetrable disguise a source of wealth. But as he was resuming his respectable clothes at the Bar of Gold one afternoon, he was caught by surprise in the astonished gaze of his wife. Indeed, as Holmes surmised, his cry had been one of surprise rather than beckoning. While his confidant the Lascar kept wife and police at bay, St. Clair slipped into the beggar's costume once again, threw open the window and began to hurl into the river his gentleman's clothes, weighted with change. When Mrs. St. Clair and the police arrived in the room, there he sat as a beggar. "Even a wife's eyes could not pierce so complete a disguise"—and it was to his "relief, that instead of being identified as Mr. Neville St. Clair, I was arrested as his murderer." But now, faced with the possibility of exposure to his wife and children, St. Clair is ashamed and has decided to change his life, having "sworn by the most solemn oaths which a man can take . . . [that] there must be no more of Hugh Boone."

The police concur that the affair may be dropped if not repeated, and Holmes credits his insight into the business to "sitting upon five pillows and consuming an ounce of shag." The matter solved, he suggests to Watson that "if we drive to Baker Street we shall just be in time for breakfast," thus bringing the tale to a hearty, English conclusion. ❃

"I could every morning emerge as a squalid beggar, and in the evenings transform myself into a well-dressed man about town."

As Holmes seats himself upon the pillows piled into an Eastern divan and meditates upon the story Mrs. St. Clair has told him, so let us get comfortably situated, supplied with an ounce of shag or a cup of coffee, and contemplate this tale that Watson tells us. We can begin by becoming aware of the forces that pull the characters in different directions here, seeing how they play themselves out in the lives of the principals, in Holmes's habits of mind, and even in our own strategies and engagements as readers.

Clearly, the pull of domesticity is a major force in this adventure, and the domestic is deeply linked with the feminine, from Mrs. Whitney, who bids Watson send her husband home, to Mrs. St. Clair, who asks Holmes's help in rescuing her missing mate, not to mention Mrs. Watson, in whose cozy company the good doctor begins the narrated evening. The domestic scene is closely associated with a sense of identity. Holmes is his most lucid self when ensconced in Mrs. St. Clair's guest bedroom. Isa Whitney is brought to himself by being reminded of wife and home, and St. Clair wants desperately to keep his respectable suburban identity untainted by the daily begging with which he supports it.

Forces that pull against the domestic are concentrated in the Bar of Gold. The opium den makes Isa Whitney forget home and identity. Neville St. Clair is not addicted to opium, but the location of his changing room above the den (not to mention the name of the den itself) suggests a link between the spell of the drug and the lure of money, which compels him daily to undo his identity. Though hard cash is typically proclaimed the antithesis of dreamy fantasies such as opium produces, money itself is often the stuff that dreams are made of. The fantasies that surround money, in the characters' consciousness and our own, offer the keys to this tale's power.

Freud early recognized the psychological complexity of money and made famous one of the crucial paradoxes with which it is invested—its connection with feces. In a once shocking configuration now almost domesticated by time, Freud proposed that in early development, children were as likely to find feces fascinating and valuable as they were to find them repellent. Adults might express disgust at the mess in the diaper, but after all, the child produced the feces all by itself— a little birth!—and was praised for doing so in toilet training, which focused the child's mastery of life in the acts of holding on and letting go. No wonder the feces seemed precious as well as vile, something to hoard, then to produce and present, as well as something to get rid of. Our sentiments about retaining and releasing feces often form the basis for our later attitudes about getting, retaining, and spending money, as our language reflects when we speak of filthy lucre, making a pile, and the bottom line. Needless to say, this childhood ambivalence often produces quite a split in the adult's attitude toward money—as we see in the figure of Neville St. Clair, alias Hugh Boone.

As a beggar, St. Clair takes the name Boone, for beggary brings his boon. His treasure is founded in filth. His dirty face is an essential component of his moneymaking disguise, and his lip is twisted into a sneer of revulsion. As was the case in "A Scandal in Bohemia," disguise reveals the reality of feeling here, for of course St. Clair is embarrassed and ashamed of the way he makes his money, as one is embarrassed about excrement, even if—especially if—fascinated by it. The scene of St. Clair's begging is Threadneedle Street—once the street of tailors (costume and disguise), now the location of the Bank of England, the true Bar of Gold, site of the great hoards and piles of money about which we have such mixed feelings. So St. Clair's own personal dilemma stands for a larger cultural pattern, suggesting that our middle-class dreams of bucolic suburban life are founded in a poverty that sits at the heart of the grimy industrial and financial centers we would just as soon forget.

Money lends itself not just to accumulation, of course, but with even more interest to transformation, to change. Fundamental to fantasies of money, basic to its very nature, is its ability to change its forms. The permutations through which money may go are many, but they divide into two different styles of metamorphosis, one looking backward to medieval alchemy, the other looking forward to modern economics of exchange. Both are present in modern fantasy—and in this story. Though both have to do with moving from the valueless to the valuable, they diverge in radically different directions.

Alchemists imagined the possibility of converting base metal into treasure. Bringing to bear all of his psyche's power—all his imaginative force, skill, and patience—the alchemist set about the task of converting lead into gold. And with that gold anything could be bought, castles in Aix as well as in air. The work of the alchemist was arduous and fraught with failures, but ultimately worthwhile. For, as Jung has shown so persuasively, alchemy was a psychological or spiritual work as well as the manipulation of materials. The true gold sought with such concentration and patience was the soul's enlightenment, and what mattered about matter was the spirit with which one approached it.[1] Alchemy was used by some as a path to redemption outside the church, and no matter how much conventional wisdom mocked the alchemist, he stuck to his dream, knowing that at his effort's end lay a permanent, radiant transformation, not just of metal but of mettle, the very stuff of his soul. Our fantasies follow the alchemical model when we dream of substantial transformations, converting our weekly dollars into European vacations, on which we not only see—but become—something different: freer, more cosmopolitan. We change not only our daily savings but our daily selves in the process.

Fantasies of exchange also cast their spell and invite us to reveries with an accent quite different from dreams of alchemical transformation. We remember ourselves as children, counting our pennies, nickles, and dimes, putting them in stacks or slipping them into the paper tubes the bank would someday accept, safe and heavy—dreaming not just of what they might buy, but (more strangely) of the other forms of money into which they could be converted, bars of bullion or bills with faces of men legendary in our history. Simple accumulation would turn the dimes into dollars. The fantasy of exchange is more fluid and less difficult than the fantasy of alchemy, and more susceptible of incremental progress. Exchange, of course, is the basis of modern economics. One form of money can be converted into another, then into goods and services, and back to money again—conjured up by cash card, credit card, electronic transfer, or check.

This fluidity answers many of our needs. But deep down, we suspect that this facility of exchange is too facile. In a world where everything is interchangeable, nothing ever really changes: there is no real transformation. Everything becomes part of an immense status quo, a protean slide of endless substitutions, ceaseless activity without real action, motion without movement.[2] Dread lurks in exchange because all exchanges are reversible. Dollars can always become pennies again, that European vacation can become the endless credit card bill that haunts us every month, and, having momentarily achieved a vision of our own possibilities, we can return to being once again our unregenerate selves.

At the center of "The Man with the Twisted Lip" is St. Clair's alchemical hope to convert the spare change of beggary and its sordid world into the solid fruitfulness of the middle-class domestic scene. He would be brother to the smelly and befouled alchemist, blackened and ridiculed, his face dirty as a tinker's, jeered by those who pass by, but inwardly secure in his work of transformation. The pathos of St. Clair's situation is that he can hope for no final alchemical result, for he is trapped in the reversible world of exchange, his middle-class respectability always convertible back into the shame of pennies cast his way in pity. And so he cringes when his wife spots him in the window above the opium den, just as Cinderella shrank from the gaze of prince, fine clothes about to become rags once again.

The path of transformation open to St. Clair (as to Cinderella) is very much a question of class. The money of the British upper classes has been cooked for centuries in the alchemical vessel of history, and it can no longer be turned back into the armed plunder and cattle raids in which it ultimately originated. Wealthy aristocrats do not work for their money. But bourgeois money, like beggar's money, is earned on the street, where everyone can see. And respectability can quickly revert to nothing but the cash that tried to buy it, solid pounds dissolving into pocketsful of pennies again. The dream of exchange is hopeful and bright, but exchange's nightmare is firmly stamped on the other side of the coin. Selling matches—"vestas"—in Threadneedle Street, St. Clair compromises the vestal hearth he has bought with pennies and betrays the wife who tends it.

Ensconced deep within that vestal's solidly middle-class home, Sherlock Holmes meditates upon the facts of the case: the vanished husband, the grotesque beggar lodged above the Bar of Gold, the gentleman's coat sunk with pennies to the river bottom. What are the meditating detective's own relations to money, to alchemy, to exchange? Here as so often elsewhere, Holmes seems to work without a fee. Though he earns his bread and shag as the world's first consulting detective, he is habitually as careless of monetary rewards as he is ready by reflex to spring to the aid of monied interests. The question of a fee concerns most readers as little as it does

Holmes, though we may assume he pursues a genial policy of soaking the rich to cover his pro bono work, as when in "A Scandal in Bohemia" he retains the Bohemian king's thousand pounds for three days of incidental expenses, even though he fails to recover the compromising photograph for the king. It is not Sherlock Holmes's cash accounts that earn our interest, but his relations to alchemical transformation and to exchange.

Holmes's work is deeply connected to the alchemical model of transformation. It is his task, his genius, to collect unpromising and apparently unrelated facts—the base material of the case—and turn them into clues—lead into gold. Penny facts become elegant explanations. And these transformations, like alchemy, are not reversible: once we have seen a fact as a clue, it can never return to insignificance or reassume its old, false meaning. In the alchemical vessel of Holmes's meditation, St. Clair's coat sunk to the bottom of the river is transformed from being proof a respectable man was murdered in a beggar's room, into evidence that a respectable man has cloaked himself in beggar's rags.

The Holmesian reader can meditate on the meaning of that coin-filled coat and see even more than Holmes reveals. Seated cross-legged on an Eastern divan, we might be struck by the way this British story of a rich beggar, his respectable coat hurled into the river and sunk with pennies and shame, differs from the Hindu and Buddhist parables of the mendicant who wanders about, lost in despair until he finds that, previously unknown to him, there are golden coins sewn in the hem of his now-ragged cloak, coins that make him rich, that even prove his noble lineage, his princeliness. This oriental parable of enlightenment—realizing one's true nature—differs strikingly from our Western alchemical tale not only in its outcome, but in its assumptions. The Eastern mystics speak of a recognition rather than an achievement: for them the wealth is already there, unconscious and inherent rather than earned or granted. The Hindu beggar is really a prince; but what is St. Clair really—bourgeois or beggar? Caught in the world of exchange, St. Clair is too disreputable to be a true burgher, too rich to be pitied as a beggar.

Holmes saves St. Clair from this indeterminacy, this lack of identity, in terms that echo a mythical rescue from hell. The detective crosses a Styx-like river that he speculates is full of corpses (murdered in nearby opium dens) and descends into a labyrinth of streets ("a wilderness of brick and mortar") to search for St. Clair, whom he comes to believe is indeed in the land of the dead. When word arrives St. Clair is alive, the message is postmarked Gravesend. And Holmes restores St. Clair to his true identity with a ritual washing, a secular baptism. Repentant of his past misdeeds, St. Clair is resolved to live a life of honesty. ❋

"He certainly needs a wash," remarked Holmes. . . . "We will soon make him cut a much more respectable figure."

As Holmes wipes the sponge across the grimy face of the ostensible beggar, so we might wipe the sponge across this tale (and the Holmes canon generally) to have a look at its true social and economic face. Though St. Clair does say that not *all* beggars make upwards of seven hundred pounds a year as he does, the implication is that many do make a handsome living. Wiping away the poor man's grime and disfigurement to reveal the bourgeois beneath, doesn't Conan Doyle imply that poverty, if not an illusion, is often a sham and that our pity is often wasted on the apparently poor, who are both cleverer and better off than they appear? If poverty and suffering are a willful distortion of healthy middle-class normality, then it is as easy to wipe clean the slate of social responsibility as it is for Holmes to erase St. Clair's begrimed face—and we can turn a bland (if not a blind) eye toward beggary, poverty, addiction, and the whole host of social ills that radiate from the Bar of

Gold and its neighborhood. Indeed, as Dickens reformed Scrooge's heart rather than his class, Conan Doyle seems quite content to let Holmes rescue the individual—Whitney or St. Clair—with little concern for the larger picture.[3]

Literarily, Holmes's nonchalance toward the social context of crime, injustice, and suffering is understandable. To remove the world's evil would, after all, put the detective out of business.[4] Still, the canon does present a dark picture from the world of exchange, in which cases may come and go, one injustice be traded for another, without upsetting the (im)balance of the whole, and the sum of Holmes's work makes scarcely a mark.

Though he may work alchemical changes on the facts in each case, in the larger scope of the canon Sherlock Holmes himself circulates endlessly within the world of exchange— trapped, forced to reenact the same formula as he solves crime after crime to please a hungry public and feed an increasingly well-fed author, exchanging one crime, one victim for another until they seem interchangeable indeed. Equating crimes to cash, Holmes muses to Watson, "We should be rich men if we had a thousand pounds for every poor devil who has been done to death in that den." It was a good approximation. The literary exchange brought Conan Doyle sums approaching one thousand pounds for each new adventure published, a strong incentive to produce more of the same.

As readers of these stories, we enter the world of exchange when we repeat ourselves, reading formula fiction in the same old way, pretending to believe each story's claim that *this* case is unique as we settle into the familiar pattern.[5] But as readers we can enter the process of transformation when we resolve each case differently, reading eccentrically, using interpretive alchemy to recast the tales in ways that will not let them return to being "mere" detective stories. Just as Holmes converts facts into clues that solve the puzzle, we can find in his solution to the puzzle further mysteries to contemplate. ❀

"I am sure, Mr. Holmes, that we are very much indebted
to you for having cleared the matter up. I wish I knew how
you reach your results."
   "I reached this one," said my friend, "by sitting upon
five pillows and consuming an ounce of shag."

Conan Doyle makes quite a point of highlighting the similarities between Holmes's nocturnal reflections and Eastern
meditation practices that aim at enlightenment. The detective
who would, during the years of his later disappearance, spend
time visiting the head lama in Lhasa, Tibet, here assumes an
appropriately oriental attitude and posture:

> construct[ing] a sort of Eastern divan, upon which he
> perched himself cross-legged. . . . his eyes fixed vacantly
> upon the corner of the ceiling . . . silent, motion-
> less. . . . So he sat when I dropped off to sleep, and so
> he sat when . . . I found the summer sun shining into
> the apartment.

So the Buddha sat, strengthened by a good dish of curds on
the night that he achieved enlightenment, and so Holmes sits,
invigorated by a good ounce of shag as he achieves a clarity he
describes not just as a solution to this case, but as wisdom itself:
"better to learn wisdom late than never to learn it at all." Does
Holmes achieve some wisdom beyond the answer to the riddle
at hand? Let us at least ask what form that wisdom might take.
   On those rare occasions when the oriental sages have
given words to their deepest insights, a common theme
emerges: what had appeared to be two is in fact one. As the
Buddha put it, "I am one with the morning star." Or as
Sengstan said in the earliest Zen text, "To come directly into
harmony with this Enlightenment / just simply say when
doubt arises, 'Not two.'" If we look at the results of Holmes's
meditation, we can see that he has had a realization akin to the
mystics' "not two." He realizes there is no distinction between

the beggar suspected of murder and the man he is suspected of murdering. They are not two, but one in the same.

Did Holmes's intimations of oneness go deeper? Did he see the reason he recognized the beggar's true identity was that, like St. Clair, Holmes had disguised himself and entered the opium den, often using it for his own secret professional purposes, again like St. Clair? In short, did Holmes see that in an important sense he and St. Clair were "not two," that each in his own way was trapped in the world of exchange? The text, like most accounts of illumination, is silent on the content and process of Holmes's meditation and reveals only the single insight that solves the puzzle. But as Holmesian readers we have the right to meditations of our own and can move into the mystery behind the detection.

The clarity of Holmes's meditation is the opposite of the opium den's spell, and we are drawn to them both. We seek that bafflement which is Holmes's base material as surely as we seek the clear understanding into which Holmes will transform it. And so we pick up the collected adventures and turn to a new tale, returning like addicts to the den again and again—"just looking for a friend" we might claim, delighting in the descent of the familiar spell of mystery, more alluring than opium dreams, more treasured than a bar of gold.

CHAPTER SIX

SHERLOCK HOLMES AND THE EMPIRICAL IMAGINATION IN "A Case of Identity"

"I can never bring you to realize the importance of sleeves, the suggestiveness of thumb-nails, or the great issues that may hang from a bootlace."

What makes the Sherlock Holmes stories so addictive? The quirks of the hero, the challenges of the chase, the reassuring conventions, the shows of logic, and the symbolic subtleties are all compelling. But I contend that the tales' broadest and most enduring appeal is based on a new vision they urge. Sherlock Holmes's principal battles are not with crime and deceit, nor even his own addiction and depressions. His most valiant struggles pit him against certain habits of mind—carelessness, conventionality, reflex assumptions, and romanticism. He champions a fresh and scrupulous attention to the ordinary, the commonplace, the apparently insignificant. He struggles ceaselessly to convert the police, Watson, and (most importantly) his readers to a new way of seeing.

This new vision turns on how we treat the facts, and Holmes is tireless in asserting two of his favorite axioms: careful observation of facts is the surest path to the truth, and (therefore) pedestrian facts are more interesting than fiction. Here is how Conan Doyle sets up the argument in "A Case of Identity":

> "My dear fellow," said Sherlock Holmes, as we sat on either side of the fire in his lodgings at Baker Street, "life is infinitely stranger than anything which the mind of man could invent. We would not dare to conceive the things which are really mere commonplaces of existence. If we could fly out of that window hand in hand, hover over this great city, gently remove the roofs, and peep in at the queer things which are going on, the strange coincidences, the plannings, the cross-purposes, the wonderful chains of events, working through generations, and leading to the most *outré* results, it would make all fiction with its conventionalities and foreseen conclusions most stale and unprofitable."

This is a remarkable, flamboyant plea. Arguing for the value of the pedestrian, the commonplace, Holmes takes a most unpedestrian, even airborne "stance," when he imagines that he and Watson "could fly out of that window hand in hand, hover over this great city, gently remove the roofs, and peep in at the queer things which are going on." This is the rhetorical foundation for his claim that fact is superior to fiction, his polemic for observation against imagination. Yet, of course, this is a highly imaginative proposition, one that would do Peter Pan proud. Founding his plea for fact on the wing of fancy, his argument deconstructs itself, undoes the very opposition it proposes to address from the beginning.

Facts, Watson objects, are the stuff of the police reports published in the newspapers, but these are "neither fascinating nor artistic."

> "A certain selection and discretion must be used in producing a realistic effect," remarked Holmes. . . .
> "Depend upon it there is nothing so unnatural as the commonplace."

Making his case for the facts, Holmes rather surprisingly argues like a writer of realistic fiction, advocating "selection and discretion . . . in producing a realistic *effect*" (my emphasis). What is more, he has claimed for fact all the marks of fiction at its most romantic: "the strange coincidences, the plannings, the cross-purposes, the wonderful chains of events, working through generations, and leading to the most *outré* results." Again, the ordinary *is* the extraordinary; the distinction disintegrates. This collapse of the opposition between fact and imagination is the revealing first step in Holmes's thinking, a step he has always already taken.

Here is the key to Holmes's imagination, and to the vision to which he invites us. His militant empiricism—scrutinizing cuff, thumbnail, bootlace—is here and everywhere founded on imagination, and not opposed to it. His empirical imagination starts as a literalism that proposes the truth is right there to be read on the surfaces of things, had we the wit to see. Mundane facts become marvels and wonders—clues, evidence, proof. If we continue to follow Holmes, we are ushered to a sort of radiant empiricism in which the world is transformed and our vision of it intensified.

Holmes's empirical imagination is central to the canon and our pleasure in reading it. As we will see shortly, it lies behind his writing monographs on tattoos and deep-sea fishes, and it even links him to ancient saints and philosophers. It explains something of his appeal to the turn-of-the-century imagination and to our own, and it shows why Conan Doyle first loved the Holmesian formula and later found it so constricting.

Now, Holmes's imaginative literalism is remarkable not only for what it examines, proposes, and celebrates, but for what it avoids, represses, denies. We can learn much about the appeal of Holmesian analysis by seeing what sort of analysis he sidesteps. Since literalism literally means a kind of faith in letters, we could not do better than to look into this story in which the solution turns on the inspection of a packet of letters. The briefest glance at "A Case of Identity" will indicate

the strata just below the surface that Holmes refuses to consider in his understanding of motive at the same time it highlights the peculiar empirical literalism by which he solves the
case. ✤

*"Depend upon it, there is nothing so unnatural
as the commonplace."*

The case is initiated by Miss Mary Sutherland, who comes to
Holmes with a most distressing problem. Her husband-to-be
disappeared on the way to their wedding, and she quite naturally wants to find him. From its inception, their engagement
had some peculiar features. Mary lives with her mother and
her new stepfather, Mr. Windibank, who is only five years her
senior. In compensation for her living with them, they have
the use of her income, a rather considerable one hundred
pounds a year. When young Mary began to be interested in the
opposite sex, Mr. Windibank at first had opposed it. But as her
desire to meet young men continued, he approved the atten-
tions of one Hosmer Angel, although he never met him personally, since Angel came to call only when Windibank was out
of the country.

Between meetings with Mary, Angel kept in touch by love
letters that were remarkable only in being typewritten—right
down to and including the signature—though he preferred
that she, a typist, handwrite her letters to him. When they did
meet, it was in the evenings. Angel was "5 ft. 7 in. in height,
strongly built, [with] sallow complexion, black hair, a little
bald in the centre." He wore dark glasses to protect his sensitive eyes against glare, spoke in a near whisper, and had a
bushy black moustache and sideburns covering his cheeks. He
wooed Mary successfully, insisting she promise that if anything
should happen to him she would remain loyal and await his
return. Sure enough, Angel's carriage arrived empty at the
wedding site, and the marriage plans had to be abandoned.
The perplexed and faithful Mary placed an advertisement

describing him in the newspaper and has turned to Holmes for more immediate help, bringing with her the packet of typed love letters she had received.

Holmes advises her to forget Hosmer Angel. He posts two letters of his own. One, we later discover, goes to Windibank's employers, describing Angel as Mary's advertisement described him—*minus* elements such as a hoarse voice, dark glasses, and whiskers that might be part of a disguise—and asking if such a person is in their employ. The other letter requests a meeting with Mr. Windibank, along with the courtesy of a reply. As it turns out, the employers confirm that a man such as the one described does work for them: it is Windibank. And when Windibank arrives for their appointment at Baker Street, Holmes produces the final, conclusive evidence: minute peculiarities in the typewriting of Windibank's reply to Holmes's summons exactly match the typewriting of Hosmer Angel's letters to Mary.

This has convinced an angry Holmes that Angel and Windibank are one in the same. He was led to his suspicion by five inferences: namely, Angel must have a strong reason for his curious conduct; only Windibank profited from the collapse of Mary's marriage, since her money thereby remained at his disposal; Windibank and Angel never appeared together; dark spectacles, whiskers, and the whispering voice smacked of a disguise; and the letters typewritten down to the signature implied a handwriting so familiar that even a fragment of it would have been recognized. His suspicions confirmed by the written replies of Windibank and his employers, Holmes concludes that the stepfather and suitor are in fact one. Though he can do nothing to punish Windibank legally, Holmes at least ends the cruel game and drives him from the room threatening to thrash him with his hunting crop. Having told Mary early on not to expect to see Angel again, Holmes does not in the end reveal to her the truth of her lover's identity. He cites the "old Persian saying, 'There is danger for him who taketh the tiger cub, and danger also for whoso snatches a delusion from a woman.'" ❧

*"We would not dare to conceive the things which are really
mere commonplaces of existence."*

So, what does Holmes stress here—and what does he refuse to
see? What gets repressed, denied? Solving this case, he combines two strategies: the inferential reasoning detailed just
above, and a close examination of the letters. As the motive for
the affair, he infers greed (who profits?); and as the method,
he infers manipulation of appearances (the disguise, the typing). In this way he commits himself to the surfaces of things
in a fashion quite opposite to the inclinations of his contemporary, Sigmund Freud, who was formulating his *Studies on Hysteria* about the time "A Case of Identity" was published.[1] Freud
was finding, to his dismay, that behind the hysterical symptoms
of many of his female patients lay actual or wishful ("screen")
memories of incest. While Holmes was discovering that "there
is nothing so unnatural as the commonplace," Freud was finding that there is nothing so commonplace as the "unnatural."
We can easily see a pattern of such unnatural affections in this
case, if we follow Holmes's lead and imagine the story without
its thin disguise, removing its dark glasses and whiskers to
picture its face.

　　Like many fairy tales, this story has at its center a slightly
skewed family. The usual move in a fairy tale is to substitute a
stepparent for a birth parent, so that a dialectic of hatred or
desire that could not be acknowledged with blood family
might be worked out with surrogates—Cinderella's cruel stepmother and black-at-heart stepsisters, for example. In "A Case
of Identity," the father's place is taken by a stepfather, a father
figure who is almost Mary's own age, who woos her in thin
disguise, and captures her young and loving heart. If such a
configuration were seen as the manifestation of the unconscious, we might call it an incest fantasy, flowing from the
desires of either father or daughter, or both. If these characters were permitted to have motivations beyond greed and
gullibility, we could hypothesize that Mary fails to see through
the thin disguise because she wants to relate to her (step)fa-

ther in this romantic way, or that Windibank acts from something more than a desire to keep control of young Mary's income, as he slips into his disguise and her affections.

Yet in Holmes's reading of the characters, there is no hint of such darker stirrings. He largely sidesteps psychology of any kind and is satisfied with the most superficial of motives: simple greed. Windibank, having married for money, wants to control all the family's fortunes. This trail of conscious greed takes Holmes as far as he needs to go to solve the crime, if not to understand it. If motive were the chief interest of Holmes stories, they would remain merely superficial. However utilitarian, his imaginative style is still a refusal of depth, a turning to surface. And this refusal of psychological depth stands for his refusal of depth of any kind: the stories avoid or debunk religious and metaphysical resonance as well.

But when, to confirm his hypothesis, Holmes turns from the motive to the only physical evidence—the packet of letters—he ceases to be merely superficial, even though he insists on dealing only with surfaces. In his militant literalism, he finds nothing of interest in the content of the letters. It is not the passion they betray but the typeface they display that provides the clues he needs. The mystery of this story is worked out in terms of writing—not what is written, but the writing itself. We can get a full sense of its import if we again follow Holmes's lead and have a close look at the letters, examining philosophically the surfaces he inspects physically. ✽

> *"It has long been an axiom of mine that the little things are infinitely the most important."*

Sherlock Holmes has many occasions to examine written documents in the course of the adventures. To solve his very first case, "The 'Gloria Scott,'" he decodes a mysterious message by fragmenting its surface syntax, reading only every third word to arrive at the actual meaning. And in "The Adventure of the Dancing Men" he decodes an entire alphabet of hiero-glyphics to read the sinister messages.

Examples might be multiplied, but there is a particular style of reading Holmes undertakes that is characteristically his own, and it is here we find our most suggestive clues. In "A Scandal in Bohemia," the first published Holmes short story, he moves from the intended content of the king's note to its material and linguistic characteristics. He draws his inferences both from the peculiarities of phrasing and from the mate-riality of the letter (the paper's texture and watermark). In a move that parallels the strategies undertaken by his now fa-mous contemporary, the Swiss linguist Ferdinand de Saussure, Holmes moves interest from the signified (the intended meaning) to the signifiers (the elements that "convey" the meaning). The semioticians who have followed Saussure have reaped a considerable harvest by focusing on the signifiers rather than the signified. And so does Holmes. A focus on the signifier resolves "The Reigate Squires,"[2] in which Holmes examines the penmanship and the spaces between words in a tiny fragment of a handwritten note clutched in a dead man's grasp, from which he determines the very characters, ages, and relationship of the two murderers who together wrote the note.[3]

This inclination toward looking at fragments, rather than the whole messages they purport to convey, combined with his attention to means rather than the (intended) meaning in communication, figures centrally in "A Case of Identity," where Holmes zeros in not on the words, but on the individ-ual, typed letters out of which those words were composed.

Now, you remark in this note of yours, Mr. Windibank, that in every case there is some little slur-ring over of the "e," and a slight defect in the tail of the "r." There are fourteen other characteristics, but those are the most obvious. . . . I have four letters which pur-port to come from the missing man. They are all type-written. In each case, not only are the "e"s slurred and the "r"s tailless, but you will observe, if you are to use my magnifying lens, that the fourteen other characteristics to which I have alluded are there as well.

Holmes has followed the path of the signifier—the typewriting itself. The content of the letters is indeed irrelevant. By following the typed characters, rather than speculating deeply about character types, he has arrived at the letters' source.

The fact that Holmes introduces a method that will come to be used with increasing sophistication in actual as well as fictional detection should not diminish our appreciation for the imaginative implications of his tactic. Not just a method, but a vision informs this maneuver. His inspection of the letters' letters brings us into a way of seeing the world that is always and everywhere already present in all the narratives of the Holmes canon. It is a strategy with a somewhat surprising imaginative history.

Fragmenting messages to trace their hidden meanings, reading letters rather than the words they spell, is an ancient impulse. In the characters of the Hebrew Cabala and Pythagorean Greek, in formulas of the Orphists, Neoplatonists, and alchemists, and in the systems contemplated by Holmes's theosophist contemporaries Madame Blavatsky and Annie Besant, individual letters had distinct hidden meanings—from the simple ABCDs of ABraCaDabra to subtle spells with spellings only the highest initiates could know. Particular letters corresponded to and embodied the powers of the planets, colors, sounds, spiritual characteristics, hours of the day.[4] They indicated worlds beyond the visible texts, yet with traces written all over the texts' visible surfaces, for those that knew how to read them.

Holmes's reading of the letters' letters is like this, but with a difference. That difference is difference itself. For rather than pointing to another system of meaning outside its own field—the planets, the psyche, the gods—the distinct marks of the typewriter indicate its identity by showing differences from similar marks left by other typewriters. The system of typed letters is its own field of reference and differentiation, rather than pointing to another system of things signified. We remain on the surfaces of things, at the level of the signifier, but surfaces themselves become as revealing in a new way as the old Cabala.

Staying on the surface does not mean leaving imagination behind. By leaving depth and attending to surfaces, by shifting from hermeneutics to semiotics, we do not abandon imagination, but simply enter a new set of imaginative possibilities. First there is the place of writing itself—any writing, in our consciousness.

Historically, writing has been seen as a substitute for speech, a less present way of conveying meaning.[5] Clear speech would reveal who is really present, the underlying identity of Mary's suitor; so even when he is on the scene, "Angel" speaks in a hoarse whisper, an essential part of his disguise. He writes Mary daily because he cannot appear in person so long as her father is there. His absence—the absence of any such person—makes writing necessary; writing and absence are bound up together. So, popularly, writing implies an absent reality, wishing to give a sign of itself.

Within writing itself is a further split—between handwriting and typing—marked again by degrees of presence and absence. Although Angel types his letters, he asks Mary (a typist) to handwrite hers. "I offered to typewrite them, like he did his, but he wouldn't have that, for he said that when I wrote them they seemed to come from me but when they were typewritten he always felt the machine had come between us." So, typing is to handwriting as writing is to speech—a further distancing, a removal of personal presence. It is in typewriting, the inscription of absence and impersonality, that the (step)father/suitor chooses to conduct his affair. And it is in typewriting, at this farthest remove from the depths of personality, that Holmes chooses to conduct his investigation.

Conventional wisdom sees loss of personal identity as the bane of modern life and the enemy of imagination. But anonymity can be a boon as well as a bane. The typewriter, perfect symbol of loss of depth, of uniform surfaces, promises to put anonymity literally at the fingertips of the individual—and with it, a great liberating power. When the depths of imagination become anonymous, they are free to flower, shielded from responsibility for the consequences. And a dark flowering it is, in Windibank's case. "'It was only a joke at first,' groaned [Windibank]. 'We never thought she would be so carried away.'" But in joking we often reveal our inadmissible desires. And it was *he,* not she, that was carried away: courting, proposing, arranging the wedding, sustaining her ardor through letters in which even the signatures were typed, protecting him forever from the consequences of his imagination—or so he imagined.

In contrast to these conventional constructions of writing as absence and typewriting as anonymity, Holmes articulates his countervision of surface. Holmes takes the old idea of empirical observation, traditionally understood as the opposite of imagination, and carries it to imaginatively great extremes. Here as elsewhere, Holmes is not just a keen observer but a visionary. He reenacts the old theological gestures for a non-theological age, filling the world with meaning, or rather discovering the meanings with which (he claims) it is already richly saturated, significances (almost) available to anyone who would undertake the discipline to see. The humble detail shall be exalted; the last shall be first. Could we but suspend all assumptions, as that faithful skeptic Descartes imagined he did, and then observe closely, all would be revealed to us. Writing a treatise "Upon the Distinction between the Ashes of the Various Tobaccos" or upon the tracing of footsteps, or tattoos, or deep-sea fishes; or projecting "another little monograph on the typewriter . . . and its relation to crime," Holmes is reenchanting the world in the same way that medieval mystics and modern psychoanalysts have done.[6] The content may change, but the gesture is the same. The Holmesian eye redeems a world increasingly uniform, mechanized, and anonymous, promising us new visions of coherence, fresh insights, and the pleasures of discovery—all fashioned from the most mundane facts.

"Quite an interesting study, that maiden," he observed. "I found her more interesting than her little problem." Thus Holmes launches into a couple of pages on the details of Mary Sutherland's appearance: the double worn lines on her cuffs reveal her profession as a typist; the marks of a pince-nez hint at nearsightedness; mismatched boots betray her haste in coming; and ink stains on finger and glove indicate a note written just before she left the house. When he reads off the situations of his visitors as they enter 221-B Baker Street, his inferences and observations quite often have little or nothing to do with solving the crime. They are "merely" demonstrations of this power to discover meaning, the prowess that grounds the stories' appeal. They are free and gratuitous celebrations of a new possibility of seeing, what we might call the semiotic vision: the sense that all phenomena are as legible as written language. A cuff, a boot, a hat, a pipe, a scrap of paper, even a typed character can speak eloquently, and the world of the merely physical becomes alive again, palpable with meaning. It is a vital vision, a revitalization of the one that drove the scientific revolution, when the surfaces, not the depths, of the world first came alive with meanings of their own.

Looking carefully into Holmes's style of careful looking, we can clearly see its allure. Holmes's dedication to surfaces has great appeal to a readership for whom the old empiricism had gone stale, but for whom depth had become problematic—religion doubtful and the shape of the unconscious troubling. Much more than simply solving or preventing crimes, Holmes's promise in story after story is that the material world is redeemed from unintelligibility by meaning, a meaning that confirms the intelligence that discovered it, an intelligence to which his readers can pretend. It is a mysticism free of baggage, free of obligation and discomfort—an appeal to one of the most ancient human impulses. It also had a good reason to appeal to Conan Doyle himself—for a time. ✳

"It is true you have missed everything of importance, but you have hit upon the method."

If the public was drawn to Holmes's methods not by the actuality of close physical observation but by the possibility of seeing an unseen world that constantly surrounds us, so much the more was Conan Doyle himself. For, of course, Conan Doyle was neither a close observer nor a skeptic, fixed on surfaces. In fact, he embodied all the mental habits Holmes battled so tirelessly. He was notoriously careless even in assembling the details of the Holmes stories, which are often inconsistent both within particular adventures (as with the confusion of dates in "The Red-Headed League") or between them (as with the migrating bullet wound that troubled Dr. Watson now in the shoulder, now in the leg). And far from being a skeptic, his credulity became legendary. Even as early as 1879 (twelve years before publishing this story), Conan Doyle began attending séances.[7] Though he doubted initially, he was tempted by belief and returned to the spirit table again and again. It would be some years before he actually wrote books and undertook lecture tours to promote spiritualism and promulgate his belief in the existence of fairies, but Conan Doyle's fascination with the unseen realm was there from the beginning.

In the Holmes stories, he had found a way to formulate that fascination in the empirical terms of the opposing camp, terms that would eventually seem constricting to him as his faith in the spirit world grew clearer. So it would be a shame if we were to take Holmes's enthusiastic literalism literally and believe it directly expressed Conan Doyle's values. Then we would miss appreciating how skillfully it embodies an imaginative exuberance and the ancient longing for a world beyond appearances, gives new life to an old impulse it claims to contradict.

Still, the temptation to take his literalism literally is strong. Holmes's imaginative empiricism is powerfully compelling, and it spills off the pages of fiction and beyond our delighted imaginations into the world at large. In Conan Doyle's own time, the police force of Cairo, Egypt, was actually given collections of the Holmes adventures as training manuals;[8] and today, as they convene for annual meetings of the Baker Street Irregulars, clusters of Holmes enthusiasts observe the details of one another's clothing sagely, drawing what inferences they may. At one time or another we may all fall under the spell. But though Conan Doyle himself several times undertook to play the role of detective in solving actual crimes (with varying degrees of success), he was aware of the limitations of Holmes's methods, even when applied in the medical arena in which he had learned them from his favorite teacher, Joseph Bell.

> After days of waiting, it appeared that his first patient had arrived: a condescending, haughty gentleman who cleared his throat as he sat down.
> "Bronchial trouble, I believe," Conan Doyle said.
> "No, there's a small sum due on the gas meter," the man replied.[9]

Neither Conan Doyle's carelessness as a writer, nor the chronic inefficiency of the Cairo police force, nor pointing out that Holmes's conclusions are often good intuitive guesswork rather than observation or deduction—none of these can vitiate the excitement of this vision of a totally legible world, any more than unanswered prayers or failed spells are what eroded medieval Christianity and alchemy. The vision is too compelling, too deeply rooted, to be brought down by mere facts. ❄

"Perhaps I have trained myself to see what others overlook."

Reviewing Holmes's methods, we see that like a good empirical scientist, he makes two experiments to confirm his inferences about the mysterious courtship of Mary Sutherland. To get to the root of this epistolary romance, he himself writes two letters, an inquiry and an invitation. In the first, he constructs a description of Angel as he would look without the disguise, to see if it is recognized where he works. Second, he compares the typewriting in different letters and determines their source is the same.

Our investigation of this case has followed similar lines. First, we have asked what the story of Mary and her suitor would look like "without a disguise"—and found that if we see through the "step" that masks the father and the appearance of an exclusively monetary motive, an incest fantasy is at work. Then, looking at the letters, comparing the ways letters were treated in older systems of occult thinking and in the close inspections of Sherlock Holmes, we found a profound similarity between the old and the new impulses. The pleasure we take in the conscious fantasy of total legibility is both complement and compensation for the unexplored and unconscious fantasy of hidden desire.

And what of Holmes's pleasure? It pleases him to help Mary Sutherland, but it also pleases him to keep the truth from her and to justify doing so with a bogus maxim he concocts and attributes to the fourteenth-century poet Hafiz.

> If I tell her, she will not believe me. You may remember the old Persian saying, "There is danger for him who taketh the tiger cub, and danger also for whoso snatches a delusion from a woman." There is as much sense in Hafiz as Horace, and as much knowledge of the world.

After showing sympathy for Mary Sutherland, and such uncharacteristic outrage at Windibank's "cruel, and selfish, and heartless . . . trick" that he nearly thrashed the man with a riding crop, Holmes seems to return to a flippant misogyny that attributes his reticence not to the ugliness of the truth but to the ferocious denial of women who give birth to their own delusions. Is this a simple reversion to Sherlockian male chauvinism, siding with Hafiz, Horace, and (to a degree) Windibank? Or is this gesture itself another fiction, a moral fiction, an embarrassed excuse for his own tender feelings?

In either case he hides the truth from Mary, and his silence sustains a fiction. The truth is too disturbing to tell. In the end, Holmes promotes romantic illusions at the expense of the facts. Better for Mary that she should feel her first love was a true love, if she is to love again. And if we could together fly hand in hand out of the window, hover over 221-B Baker Street, gently remove the roof, peep in at Holmes's library, and see on the shelf the rare edition of Hafiz from which he quotes, we might find on the same page this little-known maxim, which Holmes himself may have overlooked:

To live well we root our lives in fancy;
and without a vision we are blind indeed.

A SEARCH FOR TRUTH AND THE ELUSIVE WOMAN IN "The Adventure of the Copper Beeches"

"To the man who loves art for its own sake . . . it is frequently in its least important and lowliest manifestations that the keenest pleasure is to be derived."

The truth that Oedipus learns is more horrifying, and the truth that *Moby-Dick* embodies is more complex, than the solution to a Sherlock Holmes tale. Still, the adventures of the great detective play to a longing that high art shares with low, a desire for the experience of discovering the truth. Though the Holmes stories may not offer us the truth about life, they at least aim at the fact of the matter, the solution to the case at hand, and so we begin each story confident we will see the truth in the end.

But do we? If we follow Holmes's example, set aside our preconceptions, and examine the evidence afresh, we may find that though the physical world of Sherlock Holmes glitters with legible clues, the sense of a final truth awaiting us at the tale's conclusion is more elusive than we had thought. A revealing instance is "The Adventure of the Copper Beeches," published in 1892, five years after the first Holmes adventure—and a time when Conan Doyle had grown quite weary of his hero, whose tales were keeping him from what he thought to be more worthy writing, higher art. The previous year, he had confided to his beloved mother that he was thinking of killing off the detective. As one of Holmes's most devoted fans—and as Conan Doyle's mother—she responded with unabashed firmness: "You won't! You can't! You mustn't!"

He didn't.

He continued to write adventures for Holmes, and when the well of his inspiration ran quite dry, his mother supplied him with the idea for a tale about a young woman "who kidnapped and her hair shorn should be made to impersonate some other girl for a villainous purpose."[1] That tale became "The Copper Beeches." This story—which turns out to have intriguing resonances in literature, philosophy, and Conan Doyle's own life—provides not only a telling instance, but a vivid image, of Sherlock Holmes's pursuit of the truth. ❈

"Data! data! data!" he cried impatiently. "I cannot make bricks without clay."

The story opens as Holmes compliments Watson on having written up, not the cases involving causes célèbres, but those more modest ones in which the detective's logical faculties were displayed most fully—even though "the great, unobservant public . . . could hardly . . . care about the finer shades of analysis and deduction!" Still, Holmes chides Watson for "embellishing" these accounts with irrelevant "colour and life."

Crime is common. Logic is rare. Therefore it is upon the logic rather than upon the crime that you should dwell. You have degraded what should have been a course of lectures into a series of tales.

Holmes's lecture over, a new tale begins with the arrival of a note from one Violet Hunter, whose difficulty seems modest indeed—even trivial. She wishes to ask "whether I should or should not accept a situation which has been offered to me as governess."

Moments later, Violet arrives to pose the question in person; and she makes clear the reasons she vacillates. At the agency for governesses, she was interviewed by a Mr. Jephro Rucastle, whom she describes as

> a prodigiously stout man with a very smiling face, and a great heavy chin which rolled down in fold upon fold over his throat. . . . As I came in he gave quite a jump in his chair, and turned quickly to Miss Stoper: "That will do," said he; "I could not ask for anything better."

He offers more than double her previous salary and even proposes a hefty advance (his custom with all "my young ladies"). But, Violet says, "[T]here was something unnatural about the whole transaction which made me wish to know a little more before I committed myself."

Rucastle explains that at his home—the Copper Beeches, a "charming rural place"—her duties would consist of caring for a child whose game of killing cockroaches with a slipper endears him to his father. In addition, since "ladies' fancies must be consulted," she would be obliged to "obey any little commands which my wife might give, provided always that they were such commands as a lady might with propriety obey." These would be such "faddy" commands as "to wear any dress which we might give you," "to sit here, or sit there," and "to cut your hair quite short before you come to us. . . . [For] we are faddy people."

The haircut causes Violet to balk, even though Rucastle is importunate and her agent threatens to drop her from the agency's list if she doesn't agree. As she frets over the matter at home, contemplating her bare cupboard, a letter arrives upping the offer to one hundred twenty pounds a year but insisting on the original conditions: she must pose, wear the dress, and shear her hair.

> "[Y]ou would not advise me to refuse?" [she asks Holmes.]
> "I confess that it is not the situation which I would like to see a sister of mine apply for."

Violet Hunter is torn, but she decides to accept the post, cut her hair (though she will save the shorn coil), and depart for the Copper Beeches. She feels more secure now that she can rely on Holmes's knowing her situation, should she need to call upon him. In a fortnight, she sends a telegram beckoning the detective and Watson to her aid. On their way there, Holmes frets, musing how much more likely crimes are in the country, with no neighbors near to hear screams or condemn any outrages that might be committed in the isolated houses.

Meeting Holmes and Watson in town at the inn, Violet sketches the situation in which she finds herself. Rucastle is married to a woman much younger than himself, a "nonentity, . . . passionately devoted to her husband and to her . . . spoilt and ill natured . . . little son." Rucastle's daughter Alice, child of his late wife, is now missing from the family. Alice was so close in age to his new bride that friction was inevitable; consequently, Rucastle has told Violet, the daughter departed, even left the country. In addition to the family, there is a servant couple, the Tollers, both gruff, and the man a drunk. The cast is completed by a fierce mastiff that only Mr. Toller can control.

Since arriving, Violet had been asked to don an electric blue dress once belonging to Rucastle's daughter Alice (a perfect fit!) and to sit before the window, her face averted from it, while Mr. Rucastle regaled her with jokes and made her laugh till she was weary. A few days later the performance was repeated, and this time

> he handed me a yellow-backed novel . . . to read aloud
> to him. . . . They were always very careful, I observed, to

turn my face away from the window, so that I became consumed with the desire to see what was going on behind my back.

With a piece of mirror concealed in her handkerchief, she spied a man standing in the road looking in her direction. Once she spotted him, she was instructed to wave him away. That was a week ago, and he has not been seen since—nor has the charade been reenacted.

The scene at the window was not the only puzzle. Within her own room, Violet found the third drawer of her chest locked. It opened with the first key from the bunch she carries. Inside, she found a surprise: "It was my coil of hair."

> I took it up and examined it. It was of the same peculiar tint, and the same thickness. But then the impossibility of the thing obtruded itself upon me. How *could* my hair have been locked in the drawer? With trembling hands I undid my trunk, turned out the contents, and drew from the bottom my own hair. I laid the two tresses together, and I assure you they were identical. . . . I returned the strange hair to the drawer, and I said nothing of the matter to the Rucastles, as I felt that I had put myself in the wrong by opening a drawer which they had locked.

Locked also was one wing of the house from which she had once seen Mr. Rucastle emerge with a disquieting look on his face. Looking at that wing from outside the house, she observed among the dirty windows one window shuttered tight.

Violet felt a "woman's instinct" to investigate. Her chance came when the drunken Toller left his keys in the door to the mysterious wing. Once inside, she discovered a barricaded door corresponding to the shuttered window. Hearing a sound of steps from within the room, she saw a shadow pass across the light from beneath the door and, terrified, ran out of the hallway—and into the waiting arms of Rucastle, who comforted her with exaggerated affection and then, with a cruel grin, admonished her never to cross the threshold again, lest he throw her to the mastiff! Her curiosity and concern as strong as her fears, she summoned Holmes, who is quick to see meaning in these events.

He has no doubt that the person locked in the wing is the missing Alice, that the hair in the drawer was hers, cut off in illness, and that the man on the road is her fiancé, whom Violet was hired to get rid of by impersonating the imprisoned daughter and appearing to prefer her family's company to her suitor's. Ascertaining that the Rucastles are to be away that evening and that Toller is drunk, he asks Violet to lure Mrs. Toller into the wine cellar and lock her there. He and Watson arrive at seven and proceed to the forbidden wing. Finding no key to fit the lock, they shoulder down the door to the barricaded room. And inside they find—no one!

Holmes obtusely proposes Rucastle has "carried his victim off," through the open skylight and down the light ladder propped against the eaves, though Violet thinks this impossible, and any reader remembering Rucastle's bulk would agree. At that moment Rucastle himself shows up, calls the intruders "spies and thieves," and departs to release the mastiff on them. Moments later, they hear a cry of agony as Rucastle falls victim to his own uncontrollable beast, which Watson hurries to shoot before it succeeds in killing its master. Mrs. Toller appears, freed from the basement, and fills in the few missing details of the mystery.

Alice, unhappy from the time her father remarried, had become engaged to Mr. Fowler, who Rucastle feared might assert the rights her mother willed her. Unwilling to sign these over to him, she had been hounded by Rucastle until she "got brain fever and for six weeks was at death's door." It was then that she cut her hair, and shortly after that her father imprisoned her, reasons Holmes, again taking up the thread. Fowler persisted in his interest in Alice, and so Miss Hunter was brought down for the charade of impersonation, to appear content without him and to dismiss him from a distance. Still,

Fowler persevered and bribed Mrs. Toller to get her husband out of the way and leave a ladder in place that very night. Thus he rescued Alice, and the young couple escaped to a better life.

> And thus was solved the mystery of the sinister house with the copper beeches in front of the door. . . . As to Miss Violet Hunter, my friend Holmes, rather to my disappointment, manifested no further interest in her when once she had ceased to be the centre of one of his problems, and she is now the head of a private school at Walsall, where I believe that she has met with considerable success. ✽

> *"You have degraded what should have been a course of lectures into a series of tales."*

Holmes's famous complaint that Watson has reduced his exercises in logic to "a series of tales" may seem a bit disingenuous, since it appears that when Conan Doyle's mother insisted he tell a story for her, he responded with a fairy tale—none other than the dark and violent story of Bluebeard. Naturally, the tale is "displaced"—recast in a more realistic, contemporary mode—but the similarities are startlingly clear. The ancient tale of the sinister man who lures young women to his castle, and to their dooms, is woven all through "The Copper Beeches." In fact, we might say of Conan Doyle's story what Violet Hunter said of the dress she was given to wear: it "was of a peculiar shade of blue . . . of excellent material . . . [and] it bore unmistakable signs of having been worn before. It could not have been a better fit if I had been measured for it."

Like Bluebeard, the obese Rucastle is physically unappealing, and the young woman senses "something unnatural" about his proposition. Just as Bluebeard enticed his wives (and overcame their reservations) with great displays of wealth, Rucastle manages to entice Violet to his house in the country by promising a high salary and giving her money in advance, as is his "custom" with all "my young ladies." Although Rucastle's first wife is dead, in this displaced version of the tale, Violet is not to be the master's new wife, but rather a substitute for his daughter. Yet the clear distinction between wife and daughter has been erased here: Rucastle's daughter and his new wife quarreled precisely because they were so close in age. And Holmes's mistaken guess that her father, not her fiancé, had carried Alice away in the end continues to elide the distinction between wife and daughter.

Just as an air of perversion hangs over Bluebeard's house with its room full of murdered wives, so Rucastle's requirement that Violet "obey any little commands which [his] wife might give, provided always that they were such commands as a lady might with propriety obey" seems to hint at the unnatural in the very act of disclaiming it. That impression is strengthened by Holmes's wondering "what strange side-alley of human experience this lonely woman had strayed into." As he and Watson approach the Copper Beeches estate— located, like Bluebeard's great house, far from town and neighbors—Holmes offers these pointed reflections on rural life:

> the lowest and vilest alleys in London do not present a more dreadful record of sin than does the smiling and beautiful country-side. . . . Think of the deeds of hellish cruelty, the hidden wickedness which may go on, year in, year out, in such places, and none the wiser.

Like Conan Doyle himself, readers at the time would likely have recalled the notorious case of the Staunton couple, who kidnapped a young woman and starved her to death in a room of their house.

The Bluebeard tale turns on his giving his new bride a ring of keys to all the rooms in the house, with the proviso that there is one door she is never to open. Of course, it is to that door that she is drawn, and in that room she finds the corpses of all his former wives. In "The Copper Beeches," before arriving at the forbidden room itself we find a marvelous symbolic analogy: the chest of drawers in Violet's room (once Alice's). The third drawer (naturally) is locked, but the key she was given fits it perfectly. When Violet finds the coil of hair identical to hers, she is finding her double, her predecessor—and perhaps her fate—just as Bluebeard's wife found his former wives and her own probable future in the bloody chamber.

Cut hair has often suggested the loss of sexual innocence for women (after the prince visits Rapunzel, the witch cuts her hair) and loss of strength, even castration, for men (Samson, shorn and enfeebled). Violet's resistance to cutting her hair makes it clear that she feels it a degradation. She capitulates to this demand because there was "little enough in the cupboard, and two or three bills upon the table"—a poignant instance of the powerless economic position of single women in Victorian England, shorn indeed.

The marvelous moment in which Violet lays the two coils of hair side by side links Alice to Violet in much the same way that it connects the fairy tale to this detective fiction: the one is the invisible prototype of the other.

Like Bluebeard's bride, Violet is next drawn to the forbidden wing of the house while the master is away. The girl of the fairy tale finds a room full of murdered women. Violet only sees a ghostly shadow pass across the light beneath the door, but danger of death is palpable at the Copper Beeches, too. Here, there is no little key from which the blood cannot be scrubbed, but like the fairy tale bride, Violet is deeply frightened by what she has found. And as with the Bluebeard tale, it is that fright in her face that gives her away when the master of the house catches her running from the room.

As she is about to be killed, Bluebeard's bride is rescued by her brothers, as Violet is aided by Watson and Holmes, who twice speaks of Violet as being like a sister. The fairy tale maiden gets the estate and marries an honest gentleman, while Violet Hunter remains single and leaves the singular detective behind. ❋

"Crime is common. Logic is rare."

Like the nameless heroine in "Bluebeard," it is Violet Hunter who discovers the truth of her own situation. The male rescuers in both stories are marginalized, and the woman is at the center. Violet is as bright and observant as Holmes—and is the better detective. But searching for truth is not her only role. In a very physical way—dress, coiffure, her pose before the window—Violet Hunter herself embodies the very mystery she is trying to solve. She herself is evidence, a clue. In fact, she is hired to be false evidence by her employer.

Violet's embodiment of this relationship between truth and falsity, evidence and discovery, is complex, and we can get a better perspective on it if we turn to the ideas of Derrida and Nietzsche. In his book *Spurs,* Jacques Derrida, a "faddy" critic often thought more likely to complicate issues than clarify them, sets into play Nietzsche's suggestion that "Truth is like a woman."[2] In philosophical discourse, Derrida is hearkening back to (and reinvigorating) the romance tradition in which woman stood for a truth about life: Dante's Beatrice, the fair ladies of Renaissance sonnets, the hag in Chaucer's "Wife of Bath's Tale." But Derrida pursues the image of woman closely and shows how as a figure for the truth that feminine image undermines the very assumptions that we—men or women—have held about the truth we might seek. The popular images of truth in detective fiction are quite masculine: the truth can be exposed, the evidence measured, the facts can stand for themselves, as plain as . . . the nose on your face. These masculine images of truth are, in a marvelous portmanteau term only the French could invent, "phallogocentric." It is in contrast to this implicit masculinizing of the truth that Derrida sets forth his image of truth as feminine. It is not present, as the phallus is present, but ever just out of sight, in retreat, folded within itself or beckoning from a distance. Like a mysterious woman, the truth averts its face. "A woman seduces from a distance. In fact, distance is the very element of her power. . . . She is averted of her-self."

Derrida's philosophical image fits "The Copper Beeches" as well as the Bluebeard story does, or as well as Alice's dress fits Violet Hunter. Sitting in the window, Violet is not to be believed in by the man she faces—Rucastle—but by Fowler, who sees her only from a distance, and from whom her face is averted. Interestingly, despite the charade, Alice's suitor believes in the truth of what he cannot see at all, the absent woman behind the shuttered window in the abandoned wing of the house—a woman more distant yet entices him.

Fowler seeks to make Alice his—which is precisely what Jephro Rucastle fears, for with Alice go the rights that her mother willed her, rights to property he wants for his own. Men have long sought to impose propriety upon women and to associate them with (and treat them like) property through dowry and marriage, through prohibitive rules, law, and force. (Bluebeard's storeroom of murdered brides is an image for the dead end of this urge.) Property, after all, is a mental construction imposed on matter, and women have been seen as—feared as—embodiments of the realm of *mater*, matter, more primordial than property, unbound by the laws of mind. Derrida puts it this way: "Out of the depths, endless and unfathomable, she engulfs and distorts all vestige of essentiality, of identity, of property." So it is that woman, like truth, ultimately eludes the masculine imperatives to own, to know. She moves from thingness to no-thingness, and proprietorship is impossible. She cannot be owned or known, only desired, searched for—like the truth that leaves us only traces: the echo, the footprint, the clue.

To understand the dynamic of this elusiveness, we ourselves need to shift from man's sense of woman to woman's sense of herself. Derrida is again suggestive:

And she is woman precisely because she herself does not believe in truth itself, because she does not believe

> in what she is, in what she is believed to be, in what she
> thus is not. . . . Woman is but one name for that un-
> truth of truth.

As the heroine of "Bluebeard" is discovering the awful truth
about her husband, she is also discovering the truth of her own
position, and the need to play false if she is to survive. And as
Violet Hunter sits in front of the window, posed to be seen as
one whom she is not, falsity is the truth about her own position. It is as if she were a living example of the classic philosopher's conundrum, "This statement is false"—false if taken as
true, true if taken as false.

Violet becomes conscious of herself as a lie and resolves to
investigate the crime she was enlisted to perpetrate. But when
she, Holmes, and Watson finally open the door of the mysterious chamber, what they find is neither the corpses of other
women, as Bluebeard's wife had, or a single madwoman in the
attic, as we might expect, but nothing: an absence. Like the
reader (and like Holmes), Violet never sees the truth. It has
averted its face, distanced itself even from her, left only traces
to point to and discuss: an open skylight, a ladder against the
eaves.

Alice Rucastle, the true reason for Violet's presence at the
Copper Beeches, is as invisible as the chain of reasoning that
led the fiancé Fowler to determine that the shuttered window
revealed more than the clear one before which Violet sat, that
absence was more real than presence, that what he felt was
truer than what he saw. The story's outcome hinges on how
Fowler reads this moment of women seen and unseen—and
on this moment the story makes no comment. It too has withdrawn into the distance, averted its face.

Thus the story is a classic instance of what Derrida calls
différance, by which he means both difference (distinction)
and deferral (postponement). In brief, the idea is that (first)
we understand things not "in themselves," but only in their
differences from other things. (A governess has more standing
than a maid, less than an aunt; a short story differs from a fairy

tale in some regards, from a prose poem in others.) These other things themselves are only understood by their differences from yet others, so there can never be a final and absolute understanding of anything. Therefore (second), the truth is always deferred, just around the corner but never quite reached, withdrawing, out of sight—in short, averting its face, distancing itself, like Derrida's image of woman. And indeed, this is what Violet and Holmes discover when they finally arrive at the scene of the truth and find an abandoned room. ✳

"[T]he days of the great cases are past."

This case may seem exceptional, and the notion that truth eludes us in detective stories may sound decidedly eccentric. After all, Holmes usually leads the investigation, frequently helps young women who cannot help themselves, repeatedly apprehends criminals, normally explains how the crime happened, and reveals his scheme for solving it. But in finding the truth elusive, "The Copper Beeches" is more typical of the tales in the canon than we might at first realize. The tales treated in this book are a representative sample, many appearing on either Conan Doyle's or his fans' lists of favorites (which would also seem to indicate that their conclusions satisfy). But think how often the final revelation is absent, averted, withdrawn: the incriminating photo and Irene Adler are both gone at the end of "A Scandal in Bohemia"; Moriarty and Holmes himself have vanished at the end of "The Final Problem." The history of the passion that drove the crimes of *A Study in Scarlet* forever eludes Sherlock Holmes. Even a story like "The Red-Headed League," which seems to lay hands on the truth, leaves as many mysteries suggested as solved in the end, as we ponder the underground connections between Holmes and Clay. Our inquiry is not concluded, but deflected, averted, deferred. Typically, we end a Holmes story not by ascertaining the truth, but by reviewing the clues that led toward the conclusion. Can it be this re-view of the traces, and not the thing itself, is really what we value most?

If we see how slippery they actually can be, we may understand a fundamental appeal that Holmes's adventures have for us. Our love of these mysteries is a displaced version of our attraction to *the* mystery—the riddle of being itself. Tracing clues in a detective story mimes larger clarifications we may not know how to foster, finding significance in the insignificant, reading the commonplace as clue to the mysteries of life and death. Though they lure us with a promise of final certainties, these stories ultimately present us with an elusiveness of meaning that is at the center of our very nature. Even as we seek to know the truth about ourselves, it distances itself from our understanding, averts its face, disappearing into the distances within. ❄

> *"[A]nd ladies' fancies, you know, madam, ladies' fancies must be consulted."*

Returning to the scene of writing, to the circumstances in which Conan Doyle wrote this tale, we can see how truth appears as a woman in another important sense. We began by noting this story's significance for Conan Doyle's writing. When he told his mother he intended to kill off Holmes and turn to other, better things, she forbade him firmly—"You won't! You can't! You mustn't!"—and then provided him with the idea for a tale about a young woman "who kidnapped and her hair shorn should be made to impersonate some other girl for a villainous purpose."

Remembering the convention that a male writer often personifies his creative soul or muse as a woman, we can see how thoroughly the tale that Conan Doyle fashioned at his mother's direction is in fact his own story—the account of a grown child locked in a room against her will, forbidden by her parent to follow her heart. The muse of the fiction Conan Doyle truly wanted to write is locked up, neglected, and kept from a public who presumably would love it, by a parent who will not relinquish control. His true writerly self, like Alice, is quite hidden from view and never even makes an appearance in this story. He is also Violet, forced by financial necessity and parental insistence to make a show of filial contentment, to dismiss those admirers who might be waiting for his true writing to emerge, pleasing instead his parent and "the great unobservant public." So the story fits well with Conan Doyle's sense of his own situation. We can see why Holmes is marginalized and why the woman—Conan Doyle's muse, or his soul—takes center stage.

It is also fair to say that the invisibility of the elusive woman has a certain value in this reading. We can admire and sympathize with Alice all the more because we never glimpse her. She is idealized in our imaginations, as Conan Doyle's deferred writing was in his. Little did he know, as he wrote for mother and money, that his best self was the visible one, who sat in the window and read from a book of fiction that contained his best work—the continued adventures of Sherlock Holmes.

Staging the Disappearance of Sherlock Holmes: The Aesthetics of Absence in "The Final Problem"

In a midcareer letter never intended for the public's eyes, Arthur Conan Doyle was acidly clear in his feelings for his legendary hero:

> I think of slaying Holmes . . . & winding him up for good and all. He takes my mind from better things.

And he mused about

> the wonderful falls of Reichenbach, a terrible place, and one which I thought would make a worthy tomb for Sherlock, even if I buried my bank account with him.

Some two years after the original impulse, Conan Doyle wrote,

> I am in the middle of the last Holmes story, after which the gentleman vanishes, never to return. I am weary of his name. . . . With a happy sigh of relief. . . . Killed Holmes.

But here is the voice the public heard—Watson's:

> It is with a heavy heart that I take up my pen to write
> these the last words in which I shall ever record the sin-
> gular gifts by which my friend Mr. Sherlock Holmes was
> distinguished.

For any fan of the Sherlock Holmes stories, "The Final
Problem," the tale in which Holmes threatens to disappear
forever, is pivotal. Today, even the untutored reader, paging
through his collected edition, can infer from the sheer bulk of
stories that follow this "last" Holmes adventure that the master
will return. Still, it is not so difficult to imagine, to reenter, the
shock and the loss that Conan Doyle's original readers felt
when, six years after his first appearance, it seemed certain
that the famous detective had left their lives for good. As one
biographer reports:

> Over twenty thousand people canceled their subscrip-
> tions immediately. They, and tens of thousands more,
> wrote angrily to *The Strand,* protesting this bloody act of
> murder. . . . Young men in the city wore black silk
> bands around their hats, or upon their coat sleeves,
> and women appeared in mourning. The Prince of
> Wales was especially dashed by the great detective's
> demise, and it was rumored that Queen Victoria was
> Not Amused.[1]

But if the story might give rise to disappointment, virtual or
actual, it is also rich in readerly pleasures and delights.

Rarely has a story had such a straightforward purpose as
"The Final Problem." The goal is simple: shelve Holmes, for
good. But the subtle and pervasive ways in which all the tale's
dynamics are permeated by its goal are quite remarkable; they
make a fascinating study in themselves. For Conan Doyle created an intricate aesthetic of absence in order to pluck his
hero from the scene. Three phases of his strategy can be
discerned, in order of increasing subtlety and pervasiveness:

opposition, inversion, and the play of absence itself. In brief, to make Holmes disappear in a way that satisfies as well as disappoints, Conan Doyle first created an opposite to Holmes fully capable of bringing him to his destruction. Then, purposely or subconsciously, he inverted the usual formula of the Sherlock Holmes story. And finally, he saturated the story with absences of all kinds, to bundle away his sleuth in a mist of absence itself.

In order to eclipse so bright a star as Holmes, it was clearly necessary to match him with someone of equal magnitude, even if the antagonist had to be invented just for the occasion. To create a being of adequate dimensions to efface Holmes, Conan Doyle fashioned a distorted mirror image of Holmes himself, as no shortage of readers have noticed. Few could miss Moriarty's physical resemblance to the detective, as Holmes describes the archvillain to Watson:

> His appearance was quite familiar to me. He is extremely tall and thin, his forehead domes out in a white curve, and his two eyes are deeply sunken in his head. He is clean-shaven, pale, and ascetic-looking.

More important, of course, is their mental parity, as acknowledged by Holmes himself:

> You know my powers, my dear Watson, and yet at the end of three months I was forced to confess that I had at last met an antagonist who was my intellectual equal. My horror at his crimes was lost in my admiration at his skill.

Conan Doyle underscored the symmetry between the two when he destined them to plummet into the falls in an embrace that reincarnates the classic motif of the brother battle.

This mirroring of hero and villain has caused some readers to wonder if there might not be a more radical link between the two. Since Moriarty appears to Holmes almost as if a crystallization out of thin air ("I must confess to a start when I saw the very man who had been so much in my thoughts standing there on my threshold"), and since Watson has rather remarkably never heard of him before, it is no wonder that some readers have felt that Moriarty was a figment of Holmes's paranoia. Others have guessed that the detective led a double existence, Jekyll to Moriarty's hidden Hyde. Certainly there is more than a whiff of the dopplegänger or shadow about Moriarty ("His appearance was quite familiar to me," Holmes muses in a line that could come from Poe). But an entirely mental solution attributes to Holmes a solipsistic bent unsupported anywhere else in the canon, before or after. It is ultimately more satisfying and more convincing to take Moriarty on the terms Conan Doyle presents him to us here, a real presence outside Holmes's head, and see how the archvillain is used aesthetically to make the story possible and to elaborate its basic strategies.

So, Moriarty is the living mirror image of Holmes. Mirror images, in reversing the original, can often reveal features scarcely apparent in the accustomed view. And such is the effect of this reflection of Holmes. The polarity between Holmes and Moriarty emphasizes a new facet of Holmes's personality—or inverts an old one. Whereas the detective previously took up cases primarily "to drive off ennui" rather than from any moral commitment, here he becomes an ethical champion, ready to give his life to the cause of ridding England of Moriarty.

> I am pleased to think that I shall be able to free society from any further effects of his presence, though I fear that it is at a cost which will give pain to my friends, and especially, my dear Watson, to you.

As if to underscore the moral contrast to his archantagonist, whose very essence is the consolidation of random evil, this adventure is one of the two in which Conan Doyle has Holmes disguise himself as a clergyman.

The most remarkable thing about Moriarty as criminal is his strategy of absence. Holmes dubs him "the Napoleon of crime," but the designation is not altogether apt. Certainly the megalomania and obsession with power are there, along with hostility to the good of England, but the remarkable feature of Napoleon's leadership was that he was almost always present on the scene of his country's battles; even after becoming head of the French state, he was in the field. The distinguishing mark of Moriarty's modus operandi, on the other hand, is precisely his absence from the scenes of the crimes he masterminds—as Holmes himself points out:

> He does little himself. He only plans. But his agents are numerous and splendidly organized. . . . The agent may be caught. . . . But the central power which uses the agent is never caught—never so much as suspected. This was the organization which I deduced, Watson, and which I devoted my whole energy to exposing and breaking up.

Moriarty is memorably imaged as "a spider in the centre of its web"; yet just as telling are the descriptions that do not coalesce in a single image, but hint precisely at the absence of an image, even invisibility. Each time he tries to perceive Moriarty's power, Holmes is confronted with a "shield," a "veil which shroud[s]," a "fence" he is unable to see beyond. Deprived of direct vision, he has only "felt the presence of this force" and "deduced" its existence and shape, though this has enabled Holmes, rather spiderlike himself, to "have woven [his] net round him until now it is all ready to close."

So, paradoxically, it is Moriarty's very invisibility—his absence—that is his mark. "He is the organizer of half that is evil and of nearly all that is undetected in this great city." The very fact that a crime goes unsolved (the consistent meaning of "undetected" in the canon) is proof of Moriarty's web: every crime in which he does not appear points to him by virtue of his absence, a logical teaser to be sure. Moriarty is an absent center; he is everywhere pointed to and nowhere apparent—a transcendental signified. And in a reflection that mirrors Moriarty's methods, Holmes finds it advisable to absent himself from the scene while his own plans for the capture of Moriarty and his gang are brought to fruition by others. So even as Conan Doyle sets up the opposition between hero and villain, the dynamics of absence are already in play.

Inverting the typical features of the detective story is the second major way Conan Doyle shapes the aesthetic of "The Final Problem." Here, he turns the very form of the typical Sherlock Holmes story inside out. At one point, as the detective and the doctor are chased by Moriarty, Watson remarks, "One would think that we were the criminals," and indeed that points to an inversion of the story's method as a whole. Although all generalizations have exceptions, the customary shape of a canonical tale is familiar. A victim of intrigue, or someone trying to solve a mystery or prevent a crime, presents himself to Holmes and/or Watson. Aloof and detached, Holmes makes deductions from his observations of the persons before him, their narratives, or the papers they bring for his examination. Time for reflection is given during which he formulates a precise plan of attack. Usually, there is a visit to the scene of the recent or imminent crime, where further investigation may take place. There, or at a trap Holmes has set for the criminal, he and Watson undertake a vigil, followed by the appearance and apprehension of the villain. After inept guesses by Watson or others, Holmes offers an all-clarifying explanation, which displays his brilliance as well as the pattern of the crime. Though the space alloted to the different elements may vary widely from tale to tale, this pattern describes the structural components of most of the canonical stories.[2]

What is so remarkable about "The Final Problem" is not that it deviates from the general pattern, but that it seems almost meticulously to *invert* it, element by element. Watson is visited by Holmes in this instance (a feature of some other tales), but now Holmes is there not on behalf of someone else, but in his own stead. He is the potential victim. There are no persons or papers to examine, indeed no evidence at all, save Holmes's very generalized reconstruction of the criminal situation in London, with (so he asserts) Moriarty at its center. And apparently there is no mystery to solve. Impending now are a series of arrests Holmes already set up before the story opened, and there is likelihood of a crime of some importance: his own murder.

Far from being aloof and detached, Holmes is frightened and wary. It is he who is in peril, and his old nonchalance has been replaced by frenetic nervousness. He reports that it was Moriarty—the criminal rather than the victim or the law—who recently came to his lodgings, to persuade him to call off the chase, rather than undertake it. During this interview, it was the criminal, not the detective, who saw through the surfaces of things, Moriarty chiding Holmes for attempting to hide a pistol in his pocket. Holmes's recollections are completed by an account of the several dangers to which he has been exposed since then, all of which he attributes to Moriarty's agents, though others see them as accidental.

There is no time for reflection in this tale, and no need— all decisions have been made previously. Rather than a plan of attack, Holmes sets out a scheme of escape. Indeed, he has every reason to avoid the scene of the crime, since he is the intended victim. Once the sleuth in priest's clothing has entered the train and undertaken his voyage, he does engage in some strategies of deduction, second-guessing Moriarty in order to flee him. On the continent, he keeps on the move rather than keeping a vigil. Telegraphing London only to find that Moriarty has escaped arrest, Holmes remains vigilantly attentive and suspicious as the pair continue their trip through Switzerland. But Watson fails in vigilance, abandoning his friend at Reichenbach Falls in response to what turns out to be a fabricated call for medical assistance needed in the village below. Rushing back to the falls after discovering the ruse, Watson ruefully examines the scene that bears clear evidence that indeed the awaited criminal has appeared; but rather than being apprehended, Moriarty has apparently managed to grasp Holmes and bring him to his doom. The setter of traps has been trapped, though not entirely against his will, since he was enabled at last to rid the world of Moriarty.

It is Watson's deductions we are asked to trust now, as he tracks the footprints to the precipitous edge where the path gives way to the falls into which the pair is presumed to have plunged, locked in combat. As he reads the farewell note Holmes has left behind, the evidence seems to need no clarifying explanation. In place of the triumphant overview, the story concludes with the heavy-hearted consolation of having at least vindicated Holmes's name against those who would slur "the best and the wisest man" whom Watson has ever known.

For a story that retains the flavor of the previous tales, this narrative contains a truly remarkable set of inversions of the conventions that sustained and structured the canon from its inception. So it is brilliantly suited to Conan Doyle's purpose. For if the goal of the tale is to eliminate Holmes, that means stopping the endless repetition of the familiar formula. And as we have seen, the very structure of "The Final Problem" insistently reverses many of the features we have come to count as most typical.

Perhaps the single most important inversion is the shift from Holmes as investigator to Holmes as victim. The structuralist critic Tzvetan Todorov notes that in detective stories "nothing can happen to [the detectives]: a rule of the genre postulates the detective's immunity. . . . The situation is reversed in the thriller: everything is possible, and the detective risks his health, if not his life."[3] We are of course a long way from James Bond here, but, in inverting the usual conventions of Sherlockian detection, "The Final Problem" does have a certain affinity with the thriller: the emphasis here is clearly on the chase rather than the niceties of deduction, and it is the chase of, not by, the agent of good. Todorov also points out that while tales of detection involve two stories quite separate from one another—the story of the crime and the story of its investigation, moving from effect (the crime) back to causes (the motives and methods)—the thriller unites the two stories and proceeds from cause to effect, from explanations of the motive to the crime. Indeed, in this instance, Moriarty's ultimate crime is motivated by Holmes's earlier investigations. Again, in moving away from Holmes, and thus from Holmesian conventions, Conan Doyle here was slipping, by his inversions, into another genre of crime fiction altogether.

To experience the story as an inversion is implicitly to compare it with other tales. But when we return our gaze more exclusively to "The Final Problem" itself, we find that it is saturated with absences in its own terms, "full" of things that aren't there. And this is the third strategy in Conan Doyle's aesthetic preparation for the removal of his protagonist—to make absence felt at every turn. The story is framed as Watson's correction of impressions made by recently published letters from Colonel James Moriarty defending the reputation of his brother—the contents and even general outlines of which letters are entirely omitted from the story. When, in the narrative proper, Holmes pops into Watson's consulting room, his task is to inform Watson (and us) of the existence and nature of the original Moriarty, whose presence he has only recently discovered, and whose distinguishing mark, as we have seen, is his very absence. Holmes characterizes the past months of contest between himself and Moriarty:

> I tell you my friend, that if a detailed account of that si-
> lent contest could be written, it would take its place as
> the most brilliant bit of thrust-and-parry work in the his-

tory of detection. Never have I risen to such a height,
and never have I been so hard pressed by an opponent.

It would, I think, be a safe bet that of all the unrecorded
adventures of Sherlock Holmes alluded to in the canon (*The
Encyclopaedia Sherlockiana* lists roughly one hundred), this
"detailed account" is the absent one that readers most fondly
wish Watson had been able to write. Yet, it was never to be, for
neither here nor upon his return did Holmes ever give Watson
the facts on which to base such a narrative.

But of this mostly absent story, we do have at least a fragment: Holmes's recollection of the encounter between Moriarty and himself at 221-B earlier that very day. It is the basis for
the entire story: all the subsequent events grow out of Moriarty's inability to persuade Holmes to call off the police. Here,
in Holmes's remarkable distillation, is the essence of that con-
versation. Moriarty speaks first.

> "You evidently don't know me," said he.
> "On the contrary," I answered, "I think it is fairly
> evident that I do. Pray take a chair. I can spare you five
> minutes if you have anything to say."
> "All that I have to say has already crossed your
> mind," said he.
> "Then possibly my answer has crossed yours," I
> replied.
> "You stand fast?"
> "Absolutely."

A delightful dialogue of absence. All is assumed; nothing is
said. Yet from the surrounded silence, everything springs: the
subsequent threat to Holmes's life, the chase, the struggle.
Indeed the entire remainder of the story is founded firmly on
what isn't there, unspoken words.

Though Holmes says his presence will be needed to con-
vict the criminals, he feels justice and safety will be best served
by his absence during the actual arrests. He echoes Moriarty's
modus operandi and leaves the work to others, presumably to

the likes of Gregson and Lestrade—though naturally neither's name is mentioned. Holmes persuades Watson to join him in absenting himself from London. Watson is able to join him because of other absences: his wife is away on vacation and none of his patients needs looking after. On the day of departure, Watson himself endures some frantic moments as the train prepares to leave, fretting about his friend's "non-appearance," concerned that Holmes's "absence might mean that some blow had fallen during the night." But when the detective removes the priest's disguise and makes himself known, all is well.

The fleeing pair base their strategy of evasion on absence. They send their bags on toward the Paris train station as decoys in their stead, while they head for Switzerland. As they travel across the continent toward the fatal falls, Holmes reasserts a resolve that overdetermines his impending, final absence:

> Again and again he recurred to the fact that if he could be assured that society was freed from Professor Moriarty, he would cheerfully bring his own career to a conclusion. . . . "Your memoirs will draw to an end, Watson, upon that day that I crown my career by the capture or extinction of the most dangerous and capable criminal in Europe."

For Conan Doyle's purposes, all bets are covered. By this reiterated pledge, Holmes has in a sense guaranteed his own departure from the world of letters. For, win or lose in the battle that must come, he will absent himself from the profession of detection, and (to Conan Doyle's relief) the "memoirs will draw to an end." His mark of success, the boon that he would bestow on London and the world, would be the absence of a master criminal who would come to the attention of the public only in the act of vanishing. And so Holmes and Watson wend their artistically inevitable way to the Reichenbach Falls.

Conan Doyle was deeply impressed by these falls when he visited them. And matching his transport to the sublime was his fully conscious delight in knowing he had discovered the place where he could return his hero to the oblivion from which he issued. The waterfall, Reichenbach Falls in particular, is a profoundly female image, a cleft on a mythic scale. And the words in which Watson describes it resonate with the images of absence that typify the phallocentric attitude toward the vaginal, especially when it is associated with power. It is described as "a tremendous abyss, . . . an immense chasm, . . . a creaming, boiling pit of incalculable depth . . . [that can] turn a man giddy." Twice, Watson remarks that he hears a "half-human . . . cry . . . out of the abyss." It is to this generative source that the gemini of crime and justice are to return: "there, deep down in that dreadful cauldron of swirling water and seething foam, will lie for all time the most dangerous criminal and the foremost champion of the law of their generation." The Reichenbach Falls are a most formidable and paradoxically present absence in the story.

The last major gap in the tale is the omitted scene in which Moriarty and Holmes fight it out to the death. Its absence pairs symmetrically with the one that precedes the story—the teasingly omitted account of "thrust and parry" between the antagonists. Called away to attend the medical needs of a dying woman who does not exist, Watson realizes by her absence that his friend is in danger and rushes back to the falls, where he finds Holmes gone, apparently leaving only his alpenstock. Acutely aware of the absence of an authoritative narrator for the crucial scene, Watson asks, "And then what had happened? Who was to tell us what had happened then?" Who indeed? Collecting himself, he "began to think of Holmes's own methods and to try to practice them in reading this tragedy. It was, alas! only too easy to do." He traces the footprints to the edge of the precipice, notes there are none returning, peers over the edge to see only water in darkness, and calls out to no reply. Returning to the alpenstock, he spots Holmes's cigarette case holding down a note.

Just as Holmes's brief account of his terse dialogue with Moriarty gave us a scrap of their earlier unwritten history, so in this note we do have a trace left of the omitted scene. And the restrained tone is strikingly similar: "I write these few lines through the courtesy of Mr. Moriarty, who awaits my convenience for the final discussion of those questions which lie between us." Clearly, Holmes could give us no account of the battle, but the note from his friend does prompt Watson to imagine the final scene:

> An examination by experts leaves little doubt that a personal contest between the two men ended, as it could hardly fail to end in such a situation, in their reeling over, locked in each other's arms. Any attempt at recovering the bodies was absolutely hopeless.

So of that last grappling, we have no real record. Though illustrators on both sides of the Atlantic were not shy to depict the scene, in the text it is an absence.

Again, we feel the pressure of the story's inverted conventions. Instead of the triumphant conclusion boldly traced, we have the inevitable assumption reluctantly accepted. Rather than hint at a plan of action, Watson's reading of the clues reveals the futility of doing anything whatsoever. No solution is promised because indeed there seems nothing to solve. This is no story of detection, but a thriller that ends badly. At the end of the story, we are left where we usually begin a Sherlock Holmes tale—with a series of clues and an absent crime.

In a future he tried to insure did not happen, Conan Doyle would eventually consent to bring Holmes back. But that is another chapter in the scene of writing, not even imagined as the account of Holmes's disappearance comes to its close. So let us end this chapter as Conan Doyle's original readers did, with the roar of Reichenbach Falls in the background, Holmes gone, and absence everywhere around us—left at the edge of the abyss, with the expectation of nothing, nothing at all.

NVOI:
THE ICONOCLASTIC DETECTIVE:
OVERREADING "The Adventure of the Six Napoleons"

"The Press, Watson, is a most valuable institution, if you only know how to use it."

The problem with "The Final Problem" was that it was not final. The relatively modest success of Conan Doyle's other work opened his ears to the public clamor for more tales of the master, and eight years after the reported death of Sherlock Holmes, he wrote the marvelous *The Hound of the Baskervilles*. Since he took the precaution of setting that novel in the years before Holmes's disappearance, Conan Doyle might congratulate himself on knowing how to use the press to his own advantage: he could garner the rewards of just one more Holmes adventure without submitting again to the constraints a steady stream of such tales had once placed on his writing career.

But in 1903, ten years after he put Holmes to death, his American publisher offered him five thousand dollars for six Sherlock Holmes stories—*provided* he resurrected the detective, showing he had not died in the Reichenbach Falls after all. *The Strand* sweetened that offer by proposing one hundred pounds per thousand words for the British publication rights.[1] And so Conan Doyle set to work on "The Adventure of the

Empty House," revising Watson's reading of the clues at the end of "The Final Problem," explaining away the absences so cunningly created there.[2]

In "The Empty House," Holmes returns disguised (appropriately enough) as a bookseller who comes to Watson with an armful of volumes to "fill that gap" on his biographer's shelf. Even braced by the prospect of the public's enthusiasm for new Holmes adventures (not to mention the money), Conan Doyle must have wondered, now, whether he was using the press, or the press was using him. He had ached—and chosen—to quit writing the formulaic detective stories that had driven him to distraction and (so he believed) kept him from better things. Now that he was choosing to resurrect the master detective, an endless series of possible Sherlock Holmes stories stretched before him in imagination, all written in the same formula, all cast in the same mold, filling the future with endless repetition. Repetition was lively in the aesthetic of "The Empty House," which contained two of everything—two crimes, two houses on Baker Street, a second "most dangerous man in London," and even two Holmeses, the real one and a decoy (the true Holmes having ceased to wane, the false fashioned of wax). Conan Doyle's bargain to repeat himself was a concern he would soon address even more clearly, again in the guise of his fiction.

Six months after the appearance of "The Empty House," Conan Doyle had published all six stories he had contracted to write and was launched on another series that he would complete by year's end. It was in this situation that he wrote "The Adventure of the Six Napoleons," a story with repetition at its very heart, directly concerned with repetitive, mass-produced art cast from the same mold. It is an intriguing tale that allowed Conan Doyle to experiment with a complex of attitudes toward the formulaic repetitions in which he was now fully reengaged. Reading "The Six Napoleons" gives us a chance not only to see Conan Doyle at work but to reflect anew on strategies for reading formula fiction. And we get help from an unexpected quarter. A review of the tale's particulars reveals a number of significant echoes of a philosopher whose translated work was having a widespread impact in England at the time—Friedrich Nietzsche, a philosopher deeply concerned with the most extreme form of repetition: eternal recurrence. ✳

"I think I shall be able to show you that even now you have not grasped the entire meaning of this business, which presents some features which make it absolutely original in the history of crime."

The case begins as Lestrade of Scotland Yard calls on Holmes and Watson to present his latest puzzlement and reckons it might be more in Watson's line than Holmes's, madness rather than crime. Three busts of Napoleon, cast from the same mold, have been smashed in the past two days, a matter that does not interest Holmes until Lestrade mentions that the last two were obtained by burglaries. Watson supports Lestrade's initial bet that this shattering of images is the result of madness, theorizing it may exemplify "the condition which the modern French psychologists have called the *'idée fixe,'*" but Holmes rejects both psychological aberration and the identity of the French ruler as motivating factors. He feels the busts' being taken from the same mold "must tell against the theory that the man who breaks them is influenced by any general hatred of Napoleon. . . . It is too much to suppose such a coincidence as that a promiscuous iconoclast should chance to begin upon three specimens of the same bust."

Still, the crime seems a trivial one until the following day, when another replica is stolen and smashed—this time at the price of a man's life. On the porch of the statue's owner—a journalist—there lies an unidentified corpse with its throat cut, and in its coat pocket a photograph of "an alert, sharp-featured" simian man. The shards of Napoleon's visage lie just down the street. Harker, the journalist, is so flabbergasted by a newsworthy item occurring in his own life he is almost unable to write it up. Only by recourse to the predictable clichés of his trade is he able to fashion a story. To further his own ends, Holmes lets Harker believe that the detective credits the theory that a madman was the murderer. This false assumption finds its way into Harker's published account and (as Holmes later explains) encourages the criminal to continue operating without suspecting someone is onto his method or motive. As Holmes remarks, "The Press, Watson, is a most valuable institution, if you only know how to use it."

Leaving the journalist to write the story, Holmes takes the photo from the dead man's pocket and goes to the shops that sold the statues. At the first, he listens to the owner's theory that the smashing was a "Nihilist plot. . . . No one but an Anarchist would go about breaking statues. Red republicans." Holmes does not buy the nihilist theory any more than he credits Watson's proposition of the idée fixe, but he does learn from the shopkeeper that the man in the photo is an Italian named Beppo, who worked in the shop briefly. Holmes then proceeds to the busts' manufacturer, only to find he too had employed Beppo, a rascal who "knifed another Italian in the street, and then . . . came to the works with the police on his heels, and . . . was taken here." Inspecting the records to verify dates, Holmes departs for the second shop that had a stock of the fated statuary, where he obtains the addresses of the remaining two statues cast in the batch of six.

In the meantime, Lestrade has identified the dead man as "Pietro Venucci . . . one of the greatest cut-throats in London [and] . . . connected with the Mafia, which, as you know, is a secret political society, enforcing its decrees by murder." The smashing of the busts seems to Lestrade merely incidental to the murder, and he is on his way to the Italian quarter where he plans to search for Beppo, using, as Holmes had, the photo discovered in the dead man's pocket. But Holmes persuades Lestrade to join him in setting a trap that he claims has a two-to-one chance of snaring that very man. They proceed to the garden of the owner of one of the remaining statues, and after the customary Holmesian vigil waiting for the criminal to arrive, they capture a "dark figure, as swift and active as an ape" just after he smashes the fifth statue. The criminal is in hand— but the mystery is not yet solved.

The sixth and last bust is brought to Baker Street by its owner, who has come down from Reading in response to a letter from Holmes. The detective buys the fifteen-shilling statue from him for a handsome ten pounds sterling, some sixteen times its purchase price, and insists that Watson and Lestrade formally witness the purchase that makes the statue legally his. Then he bids the former owner farewell. Ceremonially spreading a clean white cloth on the table, Holmes places the bust at its center, as if to admire his acquisition, then suddenly "pick[s] up his hunting-crop and [strikes] Napoleon a sharp blow on the top of the head." And from the fragments he retrieves the "famous black pearl of the Borgias!" Amazed by his dramatic flourish, Lestrade and Watson break into applause

> as at the well-wrought crisis of a play. A flush of colour sprang to Holmes's pale cheeks, and he bowed to us like the master dramatist who receives the homage of his audience. . . . betray[ing] his human love for admiration and applause. The same singularly proud and reserved nature which turned away with disdain from popular notoriety was capable of being moved to its depths by spontaneous wonder and praise from a friend.

Warmed by the response of the fit audience, though few, Holmes fills in the blanks.

He had previously been consulted on the theft of the Borgia pearl, and when the dead man in the case of the Napoleons turned out to have the same surname as the maid in the Borgia household (one Lucretia Venucci), he knew the two crimes must converge. Holmes suspected that when Beppo dashed into the factory with the police at his heels, he inserted the tiny treasure into wet plaster, and after serving a year in jail for knifing the other Italian, had set about tracing that lot of figures. Holmes also traced the lot, smashed the last bust, and cracked the case. Lestrade and Watson again express their admiration, and for a moment Holmes seems again "moved by the softer human emotions." Then, inviting Lestrade to consult him on "any little problem" that comes his way in the future, he directs Watson to put the pearl in the safe, as they turn to another case. ✽

> *"Our friend the image breaker has begun operations in . . . London."*

This story of duplicate artworks, smashed to smithereens one after another, is a fascinating one. Its place in Conan Doyle's writing and its own internal dynamics come into sharpest focus when we see the tale from the perspective of Nietzsche's thought, in which repetition and iconoclasm play such a central role. Several elements of the story conspire to bring Nietzsche to mind, though there is no need to claim specific conscious debts on Conan Doyle's part.[3] The story, set in 1900, the year of Nietzsche's death, was published in 1904, by which time the philosopher's works had been translated and ambient in the culture for a decade: Havelock Ellis, H. G. Wells, William Butler Yeats, and George Bernard Shaw made ample and explicit use of Nietzsche's ideas. The action in "The Six Napoleons" is propelled by the repeated smashing of Napoleonic busts. This central motif recalls Nietzsche's famous *Twilight of the Idols; or, How One Philosophizes with a Hammer.* There, Nietzsche uses a hammer only to tap the idols and prove them hollow; but Conan Doyle's smashing of the statues captures the iconoclastic energy of the German philosopher, and many of Nietzsche's followers have instructively "misread" the hammer stroke of his subtitle in this way.

In "The Six Napoleons," the choice of Napoleon as the icon to be destroyed (first by a "simian" criminal, then by Holmes himself), the repetitions of the crime, the shopkeeper's insistence that it was the work of a nihilist, Holmes's own curious morality, and the final disposition of the pearl all provide fictional analogues to Nietzsche's central concerns: the Overman, eternal recurrence, nihilism, and the transvaluation of all values. A Nietzschean perspective can give us not only a better understanding of Holmes's situation in the story and of Conan Doyle's response to his own dilemma as a writer, but it can also offer us a better grasp on new strategies by which we may read this formula fiction creatively.

The very foundation of Nietzsche's philosophy lies in his willingness to face nihilism without reservation. His famous dictum "God is dead!" epitomizes the central tenet of nihilism: there is nothing behind the scenes to guarantee meaning in life, no ultimate standard to confirm any value. All received values are put into question. When the shopkeeper in "The Six Napoleons" is sure the crime is the work of a nihilist, he has a popular image of nihilism in mind—which includes political anarchism, disregard for conventional mores, and an inclination toward despair. Holmes rejects the shopkeeper's suggestion out of hand, but many have found Holmes himself at the edge of nihilism. Certainly he overturns all assumptions of value and ignores conventional mores—beating corpses to see how long after death bruises may still be produced, for example. Moreover, he repeatedly rejects any suggestion that he acts for society's good. He is beyond good and evil, and follows cases not for the benefits or virtues of solving them, but for the diversion they provide. And he is well acquainted with despair, the fundamental ennui to which he early responded with cocaine.

Nietzsche addresses the problem of nihilism by intensifying it, asking us to clarify our relation to life by imagining each moment, each act as if it would be repeated endlessly.

> Let us think this thought in its most terrible form: existence as it is, without meaning or aim, yet recurring inevitably without any finale of nothingness: "the eternal recurrence." This is the most extreme form of nihilism.

So Nietzsche writes in *The Will to Power.* Yet meeting nihilism fully in this way can also be transformed—transvalued—into the greatest affirmation of life. The crucial role of eternal recurrence in Nietzsche's philosophic mythology can be sensed in this remarkable passage from *The Joyful Wisdom.*[4]

> How, if some day or night a demon were to sneak after you into your loneliest loneliness and say to you, "This life as you now live it and have lived it, you will have to live once more and innumerable times more; and there will be nothing new in it, but every pain and every joy and every thought and sigh and everything im-measurably small or great in your life must return to you—all in the same succession and sequence—even this spider and this moonlight between the trees, and even this moment and I myself. The eternal hourglass of existence is turned over and over, and you with it, a dust grain of dust." Would you not throw yourself down and gnash your teeth and curse the demon who spoke thus? Or did you once experience a tremendous mo-ment when you would have answered him, "You are a god, and never have I heard anything more godly." If this thought were to gain possession of you, it would change you as you are, or perhaps crush you. The ques-tion in each and every thing, "Do you want this once more and innumerable times more?" would weigh upon your actions as the greatest stress. Or how well disposed would you have to become to yourself and to life to *crave nothing more fervently* than this ultimate eternal con-firmation and seal?

Nietzsche asks that we measure the facts of our lives by the pressure of this fiction. Our activity is not sanctioned by any offstage presence or even made meaningful by any goal. Each act must be its own justification, undertaken—or borne—so as to stand the weight and the scrutiny of infinite repetitions.

"The Six Napoleons" does not merely contain repetitions;

it is about repetition itself. The series of duplicate Napoleonic busts points to the repetitive nature of the Holmes canon as a whole, each story cast from the same mold, presenting again its familiar features: the puzzled visitor, the uncanny observations and deductions, the silent reflections and the formulation of a plan, the visit to the scene, the vigil and the trap, and the final, all-clarifying explanation. This is a world of eternal recurrence in, which Holmes is asked to repeat the same kind of investigations endlessly without showing strain. Does his pretext of interest seem thin when, having dismissed the first three bust smashings as of no interest, Holmes perks up when Lestrade notes that two involved illegal entry. "Burglary! This is more interesting. Let me hear the details." Is Holmes embarrassed to have to say this? Are we embarrassed for him? For Conan Doyle? For ourselves at wishing to follow? Yet follow we do, grateful to have before us another absorbing tale, at whatever cost to our credulity.

Protesting too much, Holmes assures Watson, and his readers, that "The Adventure of the Six Napoleons" is "absolutely original in the history of crime," inviting us again to rise to the bait of uniqueness in this sea of repetition, as tale after tale claims that we are now faced with "One of the strangest cases which ever perplexed a man's brain . . . an absolutely unique one . . . one of the most remarkable in our collections . . . the brightest thing that you have done yet . . . an absolutely unique experience in the career of both Mr. Sherlock Holmes and myself . . . the supreme moment of my friend's career. . . . This case deserves to be a classic." The claim of uniqueness has itself become one of the most predictable and repeated features of the canon. Early in his career, Holmes languished in tedium and took refuge in opium between adventures because there were not enough cases; now he might well despair because there are too many. But instead he rises gamely to the task. "Burglary! This is more interesting. Let me hear the details." Holmes, it would seem, has embraced endless repetition with a Nietzschean zest. What about Conan Doyle?

Just finished with the promised series of six new Holmes stories and launched on another, Conan Doyle was in the position to feel again the weight of eternal recurrence, of writing to formula "once more and innumerable times more; and there will be nothing new in it." Conan Doyle's reservations about such a prospect are hinted here when Holmes tells Watson that "The Adventure of the Six Napoleons" would make a good story, but *only* "If ever I permit you to chronicle any more of my little problems." The clearest clue to the doubleness of Conan Doyle's auctorial feelings lies in two versions of the author he presents in this tale. The first is Harker, the journalist on whose doorstep Beppo killed the mafioso who was tracking him. Harker is paralyzed by the irruption of something new and newsworthy into his own life. He wants to "make something of it" but "can't put two words together" until he can reduce the events to the predictable conventionalities of the journalist's trade. Holmes plants a false lead that the journalist gullibly publishes. The detective knows how to use the press, even at its most conventional, as he proves when he has Harker mislead his readers. The newspaper story reports that Holmes and Lestrade both believe the tragic events arose "from lunacy rather than from deliberate crime," thus encouraging the criminal to continue searching out and destroying the Napoleons—so Holmes can catch him in the act.

The second author in the story, as we see, is Holmes himself, popping up contrarily in another man's writing, and quite willing to lie to the public in the practice of his own art of detection.[5] As an artist, Holmes is pleased to accept the knowing applause of Watson and Lestrade, who watch his riding crop fall on the final plaster bust and witness him extracting the pearl from the shards, "as at the well-wrought crisis of a play." He blushes and bows "like the master dramatist who receives the homage of his audience . . . moved . . . by spontaneous wonder and praise from a friend."

As knowing readers who survey the litter of Napoleonic statues, we can understand the delight Conan Doyle might take in smashing a heroic image six times over, even if he had to use Sherlock Holmes himself to administer the final blow. We can give him our warm applause. In reviving Sherlock Holmes, Conan Doyle has put back into play a character who is not tethered to any set of values, and who thus can be used to question all values, including the writing in which he appears. *By containing iconoclasm within the story rather than turning it against the writing of such tales (and by embodying that iconoclastic energy within his hero rather than directing it against him), Conan Doyle does not quit, sell out, or give in but transforms a troubling artistic conflict by accepting it fully.* That is the genius of this tale. ❊

> *The question in each and every thing, "Do you want this once more and innumerable times more?" would weigh upon your actions as the greatest stress. Or how well disposed would you have to become to yourself and to life to* crave nothing more fervently *than this ultimate eternal confirmation and seal?*
> —*Nietzsche,* The Joyful Wisdom

By embracing exactly what he resisted in writing the Holmes stories, Conan Doyle recalls the strategy of Nietzsche's Overman. Nietzsche gave the name Overman to one who accepts and affirms eternal recurrence and thus transcends and transforms boredom, nausea, evasion, and dread.[6] When each act is given for all time, each act becomes an aesthetic object, always open for revised interpretation. From a life without meaning, the Overman moves to a life rich in meanings. He does not operate in a vacuum of values. Rather, he sets himself precisely against received mores and interpretations and undertakes what Nietzsche calls a "transvaluation of all values,"[7] first recognizing the received or expected attitude, then scorning it, and finally reinstating it at a higher level.[8] As Nietzsche explained in an early essay, the aim is to "dismantle [concepts and discourse], break up their order, and reconstitute them ironically."[9] Ultimately, then, Nietzschean iconoclasm is not merely destructive. It exposes the old construction of meaning, resists it, and constructs a new meaning. That new meaning, far from appearing "given," *reveals* the act of will or invention that enters into its making (as when we hear Holmes's concluding explanations, we applaud not only his facts but his flair). In his iconoclasm, Nietzsche's Overman not only affirms the strength of his own resistance to hollow, received ideas, but also moves beyond his old, merely nihilistic self. He becomes the self-transcending individual who is beyond good and evil, not by ignoring the conflicts in his situation, but by incorporating and transforming them—just as Sherlock Holmes embodies and transforms both nihilism and iconoclasm when he faces the prospects of his own eternal recurrence, and just as Conan Doyle here transforms his resistance to writing a particular kind of tale into a gesture of smashing that is the driving force that moves that tale forward. This is transvaluation.

To meet a text with such Nietzschean implications, we need a Nietzschean reader, modeled on the Overman—a reader who would resist, even scorn, the text's materials—then reconstitute them in a way that bears the mark of the reading act and affirms the very text he or she began by questioning. Let us call this person . . . the Overreader.

How would the Overreader differ from the eccentric reader we have posited so far? Overreading would not just operate from a different premise, an eccentric position outside the center of ordinary strategies for reading. While our eccentric readings have often applied Holmes's own strategies to reading his narratives, the Overreader would be the one who stands not only against conventional reading, but against Holmes's own readings, not just doubting them, but actually opposing them. Thus we become not just eccentric, but iconoclastic readers, pitting ourselves against the master reader, Sherlock Holmes himself.

Where do we turn for readings with which to oppose the

master? To the very readings he rejects in the course of the tale. Holmes brushes aside a number of theories about the nature of the crime. We can reject his rejections, taking up the scorned theories and reconstituting them at another level. Lestrade proposes (and Watson concurs) that the smashings are driven by a hatred of Napoleon; Holmes counters that Napoleon has nothing to do with the case. But who is Napoleon, and how does he figure here? Can we answer this question in a way that lets us reconstitute and affirm his presence ironically at another level? From museum to madhouse, Napoleon is the icon of the hero; and to Conan Doyle, as to many British, he is the model of heroism out of bounds—an Overman gone awry. Not for nothing did Conan Doyle name Moriarty the Napoleon of crime. He invented Moriarty in a story contrived for the purpose of destroying Holmes, his other Overman, so he might be free to write of other things. Moriarty died, but Holmes, like Napoleon, was banished for a time, only to return triumphant from exile, cheered by the public, to reestablish his imperious rule over Conan Doyle's career. Privately, the heroic Holmes had become something of a villain over time, tyrannically controlling Conan Doyle's writing, and his endlessly replicated heroic figure invites smashing.

This notion of the hero turned villain can take us the next step in Overreading. The shopkeeper whose busts were shattered insists the criminal is a nihilist, another theory Holmes denies out of hand. And, indeed, Beppo is no nihilist. But neither is Beppo the only criminal. Sherlock Holmes (himself often nihilistic in temperament, as we have seen) not only solves Beppo's crime—he completes it. He has followed Beppo's method, returning to the manufacturer and then to the shopkeepers to discover just who purchased each figure from the lot of six statues. Like Beppo, Holmes has tracked them down, one by one.[10] More elegant than Beppo, Holmes "steals" the final figurine altogether legally, going so far as to ask for Watson and Lestrade's signatures as witnesses when he purchases the bust from its innocent and unsuspecting owner.

But all the legalities are like the patter of the sleight-of-hand artist who gestures at one thing while accomplishing another. Holmes is solving the crime, yes. But he solves it by completing it. It is not just a question of miming the criminal's methods to crack the case; Holmes becomes the criminal.

Like Beppo, Holmes takes the bust from one who doesn't know its value, and when he is out of its owner's earshot, destroys it for its treasure, exactly as the criminal did. And Holmes succeeds where Beppo failed. Let there be no mistake: Holmes keeps the prize. Lestrade, representative of the officialdom to whom he might return it, watches silently as Holmes instructs, "Put the pearl in the safe, Watson," and they turn to the next case. He completes the crime of force by means of fraud and reaps its rewards in the name of justice.[11] With élan and wit, Holmes has accomplished a transvaluation of values. What began as a crime committed by a "simian" criminal has become an artistic performance, the work of a genius. And precisely because the crime is transmuted, not discarded, in the end, the pearl goes to Holmes.

The last rejected theory the Overreader might seek to reconstitute is Watson's suggestion that the smashings are the expression of an idée fixe. Holmes counters quite reasonably that

> "no amount of 'idée fixe' would enable your interesting monomaniac to find out where these busts were situated."
>
> "Well, how do you explain it?"
>
> "I don't attempt to do so. I would only observe that there is a certain method in the gentleman's eccentric proceedings."

It is a reasonable, if incomplete, response, and one that implies reason in the action of the criminal they are out to catch. In fact, Holmes sees reason not just here but everywhere— because reason is Holmes's idée fixe. In case after case, as we have seen, Holmes always discounts passion in favor of reason, reducing deceits, manipulations, even murders to calculations of monetary advantage—ignoring the latent or overt histories of passion behind the crimes he solves and focusing on their methods instead. Here he rejects the suggestion of a crime driven by passion but follows his own penchant for reason passionately indeed.

Holmes is memorable because he transmutes—trans-values—the image of reason itself. Scorning the plodding, methodical reasonableness of the police, he reconstitutes reason itself as an act of passion, of will, of élan, very much as Nietzsche does in his aphoristic philosophy. Shattering the pedestrian image of reason is Holmes's great iconoclastic gift. He enacts a transvalued image of reason that embodies all the marks of the passion he rejects. His reasoning is impulsive, obsessive, unpredictable, astonishing. At a telling moment in "The Six Napoleons," Lestrade invites Holmes and Watson to accompany him to the Italian quarter to "find the man whose photograph we have got, and arrest him on the charge of murder." Holmes could have gone, and Lestrade's perfectly reasonable method of searching for Beppo would have worked. But Holmes declines and invites Lestrade instead to come with him to the house that contains the fifth of the six Napoleons. He prefers having the criminal come to him. It has more style, leaves more gaps to be filled in later, takes a bigger leap.

Holmes's conclusive demonstration of his reason's triumph is not presented as a scientific proof but as a theatrical flourish. Holmes has become as literary and dramatic as he often accused Watson of being. If Watson "degraded what should have been a course of lectures into a series of tales," Holmes himself now curries applause and then bows "like the master dramatist who receives the homage of his audience" after presenting "the well-wrought crisis of a play." When the blow of the riding crop shatters the image so long sought and reveals the pearl inside, all subsequent explanation seems a footnote. That blow is this story's symbolic representation of

reason's power, and that single gesture sums up the transvaluation of reason's image Sherlock Holmes has wrought.

Rather than reviewing facts already before us, the "chain
of inductive reasoning" that explains how he connected
Beppo to the Borgia pearl introduces another case previously
unmentioned and presents a new cast of characters concocted
on the spot. But this auctorial leap only serves to underscore
the quality of will and force with which Holmes has leapt to his
conclusion. Here, as in most of his explanations, we are more
impressed with his creative panache than with the facts that tie
up the affair. Recurrence plays a role here as well, for repeated
adventures ending with the all-clarifying explanation have removed the need for Holmes to *prove* the power of his reason.
By now, the stories can merely allude to it, invoke it. The
illusion of his genius and (therefore) life's comprehensibility
is preserved, reiterated, and bolstered. We fall under the spell
of Holmes's idée fixe and see reason even when it isn't there,
eccentric and impeccable. ❋

*"If any little problem comes your way I shall be happy, if I
can, to give you a hint or two as to its solution."*

To his displays of reason, Holmes brings all the energies of
the passions he denies. He incorporates the crime he is solving into the solution and keeps the loot for himself. To his
continuing series of Sherlock Holmes tales, Conan Doyle
brings the vigor of his very resistance to writing them. We can
learn from these creative returns of the repressed, these vital
incorporations of the shadow: they are transvaluations in
Nietzsche's sense.

As Overreaders, we can bring an analogous style of reading to the Holmes canon, by incorporating our own resistances to the tales into the pleasure we take in reading
them. The Overreader does not invent readings, but redeems

rejected ones by transvaluing them. Rather than discard or obey our negative reactions, we transform them. As mature readers, such resistance as we have to these stories usually takes the form of familiarity with the formula and disbelief in the hero's powers or the contrived solutions. Rather than setting these forces against our enjoyment, hoping that the delight will outweigh the potential tedium or incredulity, as Overreaders we can set familiarity and disbelief into play *within* our enjoyment of the stories—for example, by combining the two. We can reconstitute familiarity and disbelief into a savvy suspicion that the formula does not work as advertised, but that rather than vanishing or collapsing, the qualities Holmes, Watson, and Conan Doyle invoke turn up in other places than we thought. Nihilism, iconoclasm, the idée fixe, and the power of reason all do in fact have their places in this story, but places different from those the characters and author would assign them, and their new locations give them new meanings.

Both the stories and the habits of reading we had set against them are transformed when we bring our resistances to the center of our enjoyment as Conan Doyle invigorated "The Six Napoleons" by setting about smashing icons. It is ourselves we redeem and revitalize when we transform our naïveté and our resistance, rather than simply giving in to or rejecting them. Such a maneuver is at the heart of what Nietzsche calls the transvaluation of all values.

It is not just a matter of cracking the story and finding the pearl of wisdom that lies within, but of shattering our plaster-stiff reading habits. Few readers will recall, and fewer still care about, the history of the black pearl of the Borgias, or the maid (named Lucretia!) who first stole it, or how Holmes connected these shattered statues to a case he had previously failed to solve. What we remember is the little ceremony Watson and Lestrade witness, in which Holmes seems to venerate the mass-produced heroic statue, setting it on a clean white cloth in the center of the table and then in a wonderful, wordless moment surprises us all by bringing the riding crop down to smash the familiar visage, shattering the very thing he seemed to seek. It is that raised riding crop, not the pearl, we remember—an instructive parable for readers.

In the image of that moment, the most extreme styles of reading converge. To the naive enthusiast, Holmes is about to discover the pearl to which he has been led by logical deduction. To the eccentric or Overreader, that gesture itself is the pearl to take away from the story, the iconoclastic moment. The eccentric and the enthusiast in each of us hold our breath for just a moment, and then the crop falls, and the gesture, the vision, is complete.

CRITICAL APPENDIX

*"You may place considerable confidence in Mr. Holmes, sir,"
said the police agent loftily. "He has his own little methods,
which are, if he won't mind my saying so, just a little too
theoretical and fantastic, but he has the makings of a
detective in him."*
                                        —*"The Red-Headed League"*

To be Holmesian is to be "a little too theoretical" sometimes, but always to explain one's theories in the end. In the following pages, I hope to provide a useful guide to some sources for the theoretical approaches used in each chapter, and point toward further profitable reading. The references are not exhaustive, but should be enough to get you well on your way into those new reading strategies that interest you. If you would like to have a look at a general survey of current critical theory, try Terry Eagleton's brief but comprehensive *Literary Theory,* the only fault of which is a penchant to discover that all other theories are less adequate than the materialist (we used to say Marxist) view.

This appendix follows the sequence of chapters and is written to be read piecemeal, as particular chapters prompt your interest in further investigation. Full citations for all the works mentioned here or in the individual chapters and their notes are given in the Works Cited list at the end of the book.

INTRODUCTION

This book is rooted in the work of Roland Barthes, who most clearly articulates his division of texts (and readers) into the readerly and the writerly (*lisible* and *scriptible*) in his book *S/Z*. But his later, slimmer, and trickier *The Pleasure of the Text* is a more seductive invitation to writerly readings. For Barthes, taking one's pleasure with a text, by giving it a writerly reading, is always more or less willed, but not exactly willful. How will a text respond, he wonders, if we read it a little playfully or perversely? For example, rather than reading Balzac's works as if Balzac wrote them, he imagines Proust was their author and reads accordingly. Such a move is not entirely perverse: it reveals not only how the potential for Proust's experiments was already there in Balzac's conventionalities, but (more importantly) how thoroughly we have constructed a "Balzac" according to which we then read his works—a Balzac who (we imagine) could never write like Proust—a limited, predictable Balzac. Barthes's apparent whimsicality shows us, in fact, how arbitrary and how constricting our own central assumptions as readers can be. To see this is to realize how much choice we have as readers, choice we need not exercise unconsciously and automatically in the belief that we are "simply reading."

Wise enough to take play seriously and seriousness playfully, in his later work Barthes often stressed the autonomy, even the capriciousness, of the reader in trying out new readings on old texts—and that is my project in this book. Even though many of the readings will not seem particularly "Barthesian" in tone to those familiar with his work and rhetoric, his shadow lies over this project from first to last.

CHAPTER ONE: "THE RED-HEADED LEAGUE"

Among English-speaking critics, Harold Bloom has done the most to promote an understanding of contrary readings. You can find his notions about the "strong reader" well articulated in *The Anxiety of Influence* and *A Map of Misreading*, among his many books. Bloom is primarily interested in the ways great writers read (or "misread") their literary precursors in order to make a space for their own writing, while I am concerned here with reading for its own sake. But in pursuing eccentric readings, I certainly agree with Bloom that the most interesting readings are not necessarily the ones at the forefront of the author's mind. (Bloom's ideas turn up again in later chapters. I treat the issue of Conan Doyle "misreading" Poe's "The Purloined Letter" in the coda to the chapter on "A Scandal in Bohemia" and consider the imperative to "misread" creatively in the chapter on "The Adventure of the Six Napoleons.")

As for the eccentric readings of which I give brief samples in this chapter, the principle that ancient mythic formulas shape modern fictions is best articulated in Joseph Campbell's *Hero with a Thousand Faces* and Northrop Frye's *Anatomy of Criticism*. Terry Eagleton can sensitize our reading to the economic forces at play in literature: *Marxism and Literary Criticism* gives a brief overview of many materialist systems of thinking, for which his appendix to *Literary Criticism* makes a persuasive case. *Criticism and Ideology* outlines his own views at some length. Tzvetan Todorov has noted that *with regard to information* the author is to the reader as the criminal is to the detective, but his focus is on the reader as a discoverer of facts rather than an eccentric who reorients the narrative. Who knows: my "criminalization" of the author may itself found an emerging school of literary felonists and create a new meaning for the term "escape" reading.

Quite often in this book, elements of a particular story suggest themselves as models for analytical tools that will best open up those stories themselves. When I use the mind-sets of three characters in "The Red-Headed League" as instruments for understanding three different ways of reading that story itself, I am adapting an insight developed by the French structural anthropologist Claude Lévi-Strauss, an idea he explored at length in *Totemism* and *The Savage Mind*. Investigating work and conceptualization in so-called primitive cultures, Lévi-Strauss described the primitive approach as *bricolage*—from

the French word for handyman, *bricoleur.* Lévi-Strauss distinguished the work of the bricoleur from that of the engineer by
noting that the engineer works with tools brought to the site
from elsewhere, while the bricoleur uses building materials
themselves as tools (e.g., using a rafter as a lever, a brick as a
hammer). Thus the engineer maintains a clear distinction
between tools and materials, while the bricoleur blurs that
distinction, using what is on the site, what comes to hand.

These contrasting intellectual styles can be found in intellectual tasks as well. The reader as engineer will bring to a story
critical tools distinct from the materials of the text and apply
these independent systems appropriately in thinking *about* elements of the text. The reader as bricoleur will see elements of
the text itself as *bonnes à penser*—things to think *with,* rather
than only things to think *about*—and will reason by analogy,
seeing the text "in its own terms." I have used both approaches
in this book, even in this chapter. To use notions of Campbell,
Frye, and Eagleton is to bring "off-site" tools to the task of
understanding, while to develop Wilsonian, Watsonian, and
Holmesian readings is to use what is at hand to think with as
well as to think about—the bricoleur's strategy.

Lévi-Strauss contends that the savage or primitive mind is
often at least as complex, subtle, and useful as the abstract
mind of the "civilized," and I am far from being the only
contemporary reader who has found models for reading in the
text being read. The eccentric reader need not opt consistently for the engineer's or the bricoleur's style of thinking but
can use whatever seems most appropriate to the case at hand.

CHAPTER TWO: "THE SPECKLED BAND"

Readers who want a more complete look at kundalini yoga and
the system of the chakras may turn to Arthur Avalon (Sir John
Woodroffe), *The Serpent Power: The Secrets of Tantric and Shaktic
Yoga,* the most complete early exposition generally available in
the west. For an overview in sixty pages, see Joseph Campbell,
The Mythic Image, 330–91. Campbell's account is accompanied

by a striking series of plates drawn from Eastern and Western art, his purpose being to demonstrate that the system of the chakras can enhance our understanding of Western art, even when it is not consciously informed by the kundalini schema.

I have used a similar approach here. Though Conan Doyle was interested in mysticism in general and spiritualism in particular and had a curiosity about things Indian, I make no claim that he knew of the chakra system. Instead, I use the kundalini's path as a way of organizing the multiple presences of the serpent archetype that, as psychologists would say, "overdetermines" the meaning and function of the swamp adder in this tale. The theory of archetypes holds that psychological forces analogous to instincts are responsible for the production of images in the human imagination and that though details and particularities may differ, these patterns are consistent from culture to culture. Of course, for the root of archetypal theory, one should turn to Carl Jung. His *Four Archetypes* is a succinct place to start, and *Man and His Symbols* provides a very accessible series of approaches for the general reader. Jung's most comprehensive single account is *Symbols of Transformation*. The presence of archetypes in literature is definitively treated in the first two essays in Northrop Frye's *Anatomy of Criticism*. The first essay in particular presents abundant examples of the process by which the "classic," mythological archetypes are embodied even in the less exalted forms of literature, a category into which detective stories certainly fall.

CHAPTER THREE: "A SCANDAL IN BOHEMIA"

To read detective fiction (or any literature) with an awareness of its conventions is already to augment the sources of pleasure available in conventional reading, though it is still a "centric" pleasure rather than an eccentric one. A number of excellent studies examine the conventions of detective fiction that were founded, refined, or brilliantly employed in the Sherlock Holmes stories. Among the most helpful are John G. Cawelti's *Adventure, Mystery, and Romance: Formula Stories as Art and Popular Culture* and George N. Dove's *Suspense in the Formula Story.*

The analysis of the romance conventions at work in "A Scandal in Bohemia" is based on Northrop Frye's highly readable and engaging book *The Secular Scripture: A Study of the Structure of Romance.* Frye demonstrates that popular romances constitute as coherent and well-defined pictures of the world and our places in it as do the scriptures. Both popular and sacred literature are organized hierarchically. The plots, characters, image patterns, even the rhetorics of secular and sacred romances mirror one another, and both point toward the redemption of the soul from the degradations of experience. Such a notion gives a certain depth and resonance to the formulas of popular literature, encouraging us to pause and reflect before we dismiss them as trivial or "merely conventional." Frye's book does not treat detective fiction, but the principles he articulates can clarify a variety of popular culture phenomena that he does not specifically examine, from soap operas to holiday parades.

My reading of Conan Doyle's relation to Poe is shaped by the thought of Harold Bloom (already mentioned in this appendix in connection with the first chapter). He has developed in elaborate detail the notion that writers don't so much imitate their artistic predecessors as "misread" them and thus escape being suffocated by their precursors even as they draw upon them. As Bloom sees it, the author faced with a powerful literary heritage must carve out a niche and protect it, partly by being unfair to the powerful figures who have come before. The most famous instance of such a powerful misreading is of course Coleridge's reading of Satan as the hero of *Paradise Lost,* certainly far from Milton's conscious intent, but instructive nevertheless. Such a reading gives us a new way to construe Milton's great poem (there *is* something heroic about Satan, something we can see if piety does not blind us). And of course, such a writerly reading (to use Barthes's term) gives us a clearer insight into Coleridge's construction of romantic rebellion.

The idea, of the writer as a misreader of precursors was first developed at length by Walter Jackson Bate in *The Burden of the Past and the English Poet* (a book Bloom could be said to misread). In *The Anxiety of Influence,* followed by *Kabbalah and Criticism, A Map of Misreading,* and *Poetry and Repression,* Bloom offers a refined multiphasic model, by which the "young" author misreads the older master in a variety of ways, in order to feel there is something left to say, something to contribute to the tradition in which the young author wishes to work. The six phases he proposes, and the cabalistic subtlety with which he develops them, would provide a far more elaborate machinery than is needed in the present case. Still, the idea of influence not as copying but as misreading is one very much at play in my look at the relation between Poe and Conan Doyle, which perfectly embodies the act of imitating one's precursor by seeming to misunderstand him.

CHAPTER FOUR: *A STUDY IN SCARLET*

Using Jung's psychology rather than Freud's and focusing on Jung's typology rather than his theory of archetypes may seem slightly off-center, but the radical eccentricity here is treating the psyches of whole literary works rather than their individual characters or their authors, a move that leaves me standing almost alone (so far) with no list of in-depth sources to recommend to you beyond writers interested in the *political* unconscious, such as Fredric Jameson. Readers interested in pursuing a psychological understanding grounded in Conan Doyle's life would do well to consult Owen Dudley Edwards's biographical study, *The Quest for Sherlock Holmes.*

Jung's briefest discussion of the four psychological functions is found in *Man and His Symbols.* The classic account is his *Psychological Types,* a fascinating read. Though the subsequent literature on the subject is voluminous, perhaps the most useful addition is *Jung's Typology.* In it, Jung's coworker and friend Marie-Louise von Franz presents several lectures on "The Inferior Function." Rather than focusing, as Jung did, on the attitude generated by the dominant function, von Franz characterizes the inferior function of each type and explores the way it impinges on behavior—the strategy I use to read *A Study in Scarlet*.

Von Franz is also the author of *Patterns of Creativity Mirrored in Creation Myths*, which examines in great depth the foundation stories of a number of cultures. Her many insights include the observation that creation myths also symbolize the processes of coming to consciousness, though that observation is not new with her. In discussing evolving consciousness, I combine and integrate Freudian and Jungian stages, a move that might start index fingers of either school's orthodox wagging, but it is a strategy that has its roots in such psychological classics as Erich Neumann's *Origins and History of Consciousness* and one with which such eminent current practitioners as James Hillman have had considerable success. *Re-Visioning Psychology* outlines the basis for Hillman's work.

The notion that texts contradict their own basic categories is fundamental to deconstruction, though that is not the approach I take here. (For an indication of the most helpful texts on that movement, see the sections of the appendix that cover "The Final Problem" and "The Adventure of the Copper Beeches.") Deconstruction itself can (and should) be psychologized as a well-defended verbal assault on the authority of the father (the *T*ext), but that is another chapter of another book.

CHAPTER FIVE: "THE MAN WITH THE TWISTED LIP"

Alchemy has had a very checkered reputation in the history of ideas. Chaucer satirized alchemists in the *Canon's Yeoman's Tale*, and in *The Alchemists* Ben Jonson mocked their lust for precious metal and their folly in thinking they could make gold from lead. But in fact a great many good and intelligent people used alchemy not as a way to get rich, but as a metaphysical discipline that recognized the sacred potential in matter and connected one's soul sacramentally to the physical world. Isaac Newton developed his theory of universal gravitation while he still practiced alchemy, and he originally expressed the theory of gravity in terms consonant with the alchemical vision, only shifting ground and moving away from alchemy when public pressure to conform to the materialist scientific establishment became too strong to resist. (For an excellent history of Newton's relation to alchemy, see Morris Berman's *The Reenchantment of the World,* which uses alchemy to talk about ways of getting past the cul-de-sac of the body-mind dualism to which positive science has finally led us.)

Practicing alchemists still exist, remarkably enough. A good illustrated introduction by a twentieth-century alchemist is Stanislas Klossowski de Rola's *Alchemy: The Secret Art.* But perhaps the most famous twentieth-century treatment of alchemy is Carl Jung's. His last full-length work, *Mysterium Conjunctionis,* elucidates alchemy as a symbolic system that outlines the stages of psychological individuation (rather than treating metallic chemistry). In this century, Jung has done the most to redeem alchemy for serious intellectual inquiry. A good brief collection of reflections on money by Jung's followers can be found in *Soul and Money.*

Freud, in effect, performed reverse alchemy in turning money into feces. Among Freudians, Norman O. Brown has given the most complete psychoanalytic account of money in his remarkable book *Life Against Death,* in the section entitled "Filthy Lucre." Brown, however, does not see the distinction I draw here between exchange and alchemy, and so equates the two, calling alchemy protocapitalism.

Those interested in the nondualistic teaching of Buddhism to which I allude at the end of this chapter may find the *Hsin Hsin Ming* of the third Zen patriarch Sengtsan best translated by Richard B. Clarke as "Verses on the Faith Mind" in Jack Kornfield's collection *Teachings of the Buddha.* The Buddha's own enlightenment experience is well recounted in Thich Nhat Hanh's *Old Path White Clouds: Walking in the Footsteps of the Buddha.* And an excellent explanation of nondualistic enlightenment can be found in Shunryu Suzuki's *Zen Mind, Beginner's Mind.*

CHAPTER SIX: "A CASE OF IDENTITY"

Ferdinand de Saussure's ideas about the signifier and signified are at the root of modern semiotics, and they are most accessibly presented in Jonathan Culler's *Ferdinand de Saussure* and Terence Hawkes's *Structuralism and Semiotics,* though practically any book having to do with structuralism will give an account of his basic tenets. Saussure's theories have now been applied not only to language and literature but to systems of signification as diverse as fashion, political posters, and wrestling matches—always with attention to the signifiers as well as the purportedly signified. See, for example, Roland Barthes's *Mythologies,* which is devoted to the semiotics of popular culture.

Derrida, whose philosophical deconstruction is an extension and critique of Saussure's structuralism, launched himself into public awareness with *Of Grammatology,* first published in French in 1967, and in English in 1976. Among the many innovations he sets forth there is the notion that writing, rather than being a signifier for speech (the absent signified), is in fact more primary than speech. Rather than joining the philosophical debate, I have simply noted that the common-sense view (that speech is more primary than writing) is the one that seems to govern the place of writing in "A Case of Identity." A good, readable overview of Derrida's theory of writing (and his philosophy generally) can be found in Jonathan Culler's *On Deconstruction.* The topic of difference, briefly alluded to in the analysis of the present story, comes into play in the chapter on "The Copper Beeches."

My examination of Conan Doyle's paradoxical ability to express his own otherworldly mystical impulses in what looks like empiricism rests on an understanding of the ways in which the psyche repeats its central formula in radically diverse forms, territory most compellingly explored by Kenneth Burke and Norman Holland. Holland, better known as a theorist of reader response, persuasively demonstrates the ways in which a writer rings changes on a constant identity theme in his analysis of the poetry of H.D., which can be found in the first section of his compact and elegant book *Poems in Persons.* Kenneth Burke's *Counter-Statement* offers his clearest schematic explanation of how an author can use a single symbolic formula to embody and shape various—even contradictory—materials.

CHAPTER SEVEN: "THE COPPER BEECHES"

Freud used the term *displacement* to describe the tendency of the dream and tale to transform psychologically difficult material into forms consciousness could accept. So, anger at the mother is directed instead toward the familiar wicked stepmother, who arrives on the scene after the good mother passes away. Displacement, as used by literary critics, occurs when "a symbol of life energy [is] stepped down to the requirements of a certain specific case," as Joseph Campbell put it in *The Hero with a Thousand Faces.* Northrop Frye explains the concept most fully in the first essay of his *Anatomy of Criticism* as the tendency for fantastic mythic stories, characters, and symbols to turn up in relatively more "realistic" fiction, the extravagantly imaginative elements tamed to believability. Rather than dispelling myth with realism, displacement accommodates the two. Though not particularly realistic in itself, the serpent in "The Speckled Band" is a displaced version of the hoard-guarding dragon, since a swamp adder is more believable (these days) than its medieval original. The story of Bluebeard does not have many fantastic elements (the bloody key is purged entirely from "The Copper Beeches"), but displacement is still in operation, as the motifs of the original story are reincarnated in the economic and social contexts in which independent young women might find themselves in Victorian England.

As for the elements of deconstruction used in this chapter, the best exposition of Derrida's complex attitude toward the feminine is *Spurs* itself. Derrida gives his most accessible vision of his own positions in *Positions,* a brief, conversational introduction to the basic strategies of deconstruction by its past and present master. For a more complete exposition of his thought, begin with the long and complex *Of Grammatology*. Derrida is complex enough to need commentators and fortunate enough to have attracted good ones. Among the best and most accessible explications of his thought and the movement he has defined is Jonathan Culler's *On Deconstruction*, already mentioned in the appendix to the previous chapter. Equally good is Vincent Leitch's *Deconstructive Criticism: An Advanced Introduction*.

CHAPTER EIGHT: "THE FINAL PROBLEM"

Each of the three stages analyzing "The Final Problem" is rooted in a different type of theory. To address the first stage, the most interesting way to understand characterological opposition is Jung's theory of the shadow, most succinctly expressed in his *Aion: Phenomenology of the Self*. The variety and implications of the different ways the shadow can function in stories is marvelously unpacked in Marie-Louise von Franz's *Shadow and Evil in Fairy Tales*. Since the shadow consists of what the ego denies about its own being, it curiously completes the picture of the ego as well as contrasts to it—as is clear not only in Holmes's relation to Moriarty, but also in Lear's to the fool, Gatsby's to Wolfsheim, Dimmesdale's to Chillingsworth, and Huck's to Jim. Since in psychology the shadow is a constituent of the psyche, one might treat literary shadows as psychological projections of the protagonists. But as Jung and von Franz point out, our shadows are often projected onto (and revealed in our relations to) real people; and so within the compass of this story, I treat Moriarty as a character separate from Holmes.

When we move from one character who mirrors another (both reversing and reflecting him) to a plot that inverts the usual conventions of the detective story formula, we have entered the territory of literary satire, broadly understood. As Northrop Frye elaborates the term in the third essay of his *Anatomy of Criticism*, satire describes a structural inversion of the conventions of romance and is closely related to the literary anatomy, often revealing systematically the properties of the original in the process of inversion. Like comedy (Dante is the obvious example), satire need not be funny, though it may be (as in the repartee of Holmes and Moriarty). Tzvetan Todorov's essay does not recognize the satiric relation between the detective story and the thriller, but it is there nevertheless.

A concern with absence is the hallmark of many current critics and philosophers, who seem particularly fascinated with gaps, abysses, margins, and vacancies. A good overview of the shape of emptiness in literary criticism may be found in Vincent Leitch's *Deconstructive Criticism: An Advanced Introduction,* and the place of absence in postmodern art and culture generally may be profitably explored in a book such as Ihab Hassan's *The Postmodern Turn.* Absences have figured in my own treatments of the Holmes stories early and late—starting with the tap in "The Red-Headed League," with which Holmes determines the absence of a tunnel in front of the pawnshop, and turning up as recently as the always missing Alice Rucastle in "The Copper Beeches." But absence itself is most thoroughly thematized in this story that Conan Doyle designed to absent his hero from the scene.

CHAPTER NINE: "THE SIX NAPOLEONS"

Reading Nietzsche is exhilarating because his aphoristic outrageousness can force you to realize that you are not only constructing a philosopher to whom to attribute these often contradictory remarks, but are also constructing a version of yourself as reader who responds to and resists them. Good places to begin include *The Twilight of the Idols, The Joyful Wisdom,* or *Ecce Homo.* The selections Walter Kaufmann chose for *The Portable Nietzsche* provide an excellent sampling. J. P. Stern's *Friedrich Nietzsche* is a good, synoptic introduction to his thought.

A number of Nietzschean ideas ambient in Conan Doyle's culture are very much alive and kicking today in various guises and transmutations. Daniel O'Hara's collection of essays entitled *Why Nietzsche Now?* makes a good faith effort to answer the question its title poses and is useful in setting the philosopher in the contemporary scene. Among the most useful surveys of Nietzsche's influence is a pair of chapters in Christopher Norris's *Deconstruction: Theory & Practice.* Harold Bloom's work with misreading owes a great deal to Nietzsche, though he stresses its other roots. (See my other comments on Bloom in the sections of this appendix for chapters 1 and 3.)

I would claim for ordinary readers the pleasures Bloom assigns to great writers—the ability to create strong and interesting "(mis)readings" of canonical texts. Once we realize that there is no "natural" or "neutral" reading, we can go about making our readings as interesting as possible—an enterprise I hope this book encourages you to undertake, now that you have finished with my eccentric readings of the adventures of Sherlock Holmes.

Notes

Introduction

1. A recent casebook of critical essays I have used in the classroom illustrates the problem. *The Purloined Poe* contains, in addition to the twenty-seven page text of Lacan's discourse on the tale, forty-three pages of "Overview," "Map of the Text," and "Notes to the Text," the sole and necessary mission of which is to make Lacan intelligible to already careful readers—all quite in addition to the *responses* to Lacan by Derrida (whose forty-page essay requires a mere dozen pages of introduction) and others. The insights afforded in these essays are sometimes remarkable, but not always so remarkable as the obscurity of the prose would suggest. Poe's story, and some of Lacan's responses to it, I treat in the coda to chapter 3, on "A Scandal in Bohemia." (Complete bibliographical information on Lacan's seminar and all other works I cite can be found in the list of works cited.)

Chapter 2

1. Baring-Gould, *The Annotated Sherlock Holmes,* 1:266.
2. Shankara, *Crest-Jewel of Discrimination (Viveka-Chudamani),* 90–91.
3. In heading for India, which figured in more than a dozen of Conan Doyle's stories, I realize we are skipping over the Levant and the possibility of a biblical interpretation. Certainly an Edenic parallel might be tempting, with a Satanic Dr. Roylott bringing physical rather than spiritual death to a young woman by means of a snake in the midst of his fallen estate. However, the woman in question is not tempted but frightened and repelled. An Adam (her fiancé?) seems rather far off stage, though Holmes might well serve as a Christological figure, arriving late in the story, just in time to effect a salvation. In all, such a line of argument would be much less comprehensive and satisfying than the more geographically eccentric Indian proposition I would like to put forth. Readers interested in Old and New Testament parallels in the

Holmes stories should consult Wayne Wall, *God and Sherlock Holmes: A Study in the Life and Literature of Arthur Conan Doyle.*

4. See *The Annotated Sherlock Holmes,* 1:246.

CHAPTER 3

1. Holmes had appeared in two novels—*A Study in Scarlet* (1887) and *The Sign of the Four* (1890)—before "A Scandal in Bohemia" graced the July 1891 issue of the *Strand Magazine,* the first Holmes short story of the many to be published in that periodical.

2. *The Secular Scripture: A Study of the Structure of Romance,* 73.

3. Frye, 73, 76, 86.

4. A Jungian reading would suggest that the principal female character in a story with a male hero is often an anima figure—an outer embodiment or reflection of the hero's soul. Certainly the shifts in Adler's fate and standing echo changes in Holmes, and vice versa. As Holmes recognizes Adler's worth, he honors the integrity of his own soul.

5. Conan Doyle himself was no stranger to a Victorian ethos combining idealized love and sexual repression. In 1896, five years after writing this story, and already married to Louise for eleven years, he fell completely in love with Jean Leckie and she with him. But he remained physically faithful to Louise until her death ten years later, after which he married Jean (who, incidentally, like Irene Adler sang opera).

6. I focus here on reversals. There are of course other differences that are not inversions (for example, the police are involved in Poe's tale but not in Conan Doyle's; the French royal marriage is already accomplished, the Bohemian, pending). And there are as well other similarities that link the two stories (for example, both Dupin and Holmes survey the rooms of their antagonists by pretending some infirmity). But it is the reversals that most clearly reveal the particular nature of Conan Doyle's debt to Poe.

7. Lacan's "Seminar on 'The Purloined Letter'" has been widely reprinted and is most usefully located amid abundant explanatory apparatus and commentaries in *The Purloined Poe,* the casebook already mentioned in the notes to the Introduction. Those familiar with the arguments Lacan derives from Poe's story will see how different his psychological generalizations might have been if "A Scandal in Bohemia" had served as his model.

8. Lacan posits a third scene, one in which the minister is blind to what is going on, Dupin sees but does not see that he is seen, and the

reader/critic (Lacan himself) sees and takes advantage of it. To extend his principle, we are in a position to see what Lacan does not, because we have read, as Lacan has not, the reversed letter, "A Scandal in Bohemia."

9. Lacan concurs that there is a lot of smoke blown in Dupin's "parade of erudition" but contends it reveals a key to the story—as if a magician is really explaining his trick to us, without our seeing a thing. Dupin's principle that what is written large is often hardest to discern (observable in letters spaced widely across a map) Lacan applies to the configuration of the letter's "hiding place." In search of the feminine in the minister's unconscious, he finds that the card rack bearing the letter, the focus of all our interest, hangs from a clitoral knob between the very feminine "cheeks of the fireplace." Thus Lacan claims the female body is writ large across the surface of the story and goes largely undetected. A similar reading could, of course, be given to the symbolic hymen that must be preserved if Irene Adler's "virginity" is to remain intact: it is a bit of film located in a recess in her sitting room.

CHAPTER 4

1. The sweep of Conan Doyle's romantic imagination is evident here. As William Baring-Gould reports, Brigham Young's own account put the number at fewer than 150.

2. *Man and His Symbols,* 49.

3. Dr. Watson (or Dr. Conan Doyle) also turns his face from the sexual element, even as he introduces its results. Jefferson Hope died from aortic aneurism, a condition caused almost exclusively by syphilis, as a number of researchers have pointed out and as *In Bed with Sherlock Holmes* and *The Annotated Sherlock Holmes* have adequately documented. That Watson would accept Hope's attribution of the condition to "overexposure and under-feeding" speaks of discretion or squeamishness rather than his (and Conan Doyle's) medical training. This is another case of the text's suppressing an unconscious element involving passion while allowing its symptom to figure prominently in the consciousness of the frame narrative.

4. For a look at how the elements of romance can be transformed by the detective story form (not just embedded in it by repression), see the chapter on "A Scandal in Bohemia."

5. For the proposition that Holmes's militant empiricism itself becomes a kind of faith and even has mystical possibilities, have a look at the chapter on "A Case of Identity."

6. The Mormon melodrama does eventually come to Holmes's attention. After the case was closed and the account written, Holmes read *A Study in Scarlet*. At the beginning of *The Sign of Four*, he chastises Watson for the sort of excess we have seen in part 2.

> "I glanced over it," said he. "Honestly, I cannot congratulate you upon it. Detection is, or ought to be, an exact science, and should be treated in the same cold and unemotional manner. You have attempted to tinge it with romanticism, which produces much the same effect as if you worked a love-story or an elopement into the fifth proposition of Euclid."
>
> "But the romance was there," I remonstrated. "I could not tamper with the facts."
>
> "*Some facts should be suppressed,* or, at least, a just sense of proportion should be observed in treating them. The only point in the case which deserved mention was the curious analytical reasoning from effect to causes, by which I succeeded in unravelling it."
>
> I was annoyed at this criticism of a work which had been specially designed to please him. I confess, too, that I was irritated by the egotism which seemed to demand that every line of my pamphlet should be devoted to his own special doings. [my emphasis]

Though Holmes has become aware of the facts of the case, he still rejects the emotions that accompany them. In suggesting that "some facts should be suppressed" in the service of maintaining a "cold and emotional manner," he indicates how far he is willing to go in drawing a clear line between conscious and unconscious values. His remarks on proportion and manner indicate that he found the emotionally charged style as inferior as he found the content. Like the rest of his consciously held ideas and methods, Holmes's literary opinions favor the suppression of feeling.

7. Although Holmes never senses he is guided by divine justice, as the stories accumulate he becomes increasingly nonchalant toward questions of law, letting criminals escape punishment if he deems their cause just or their suffering already sufficient. And he not only settles scores with old enemies such as John Clay, but undertakes an apparently self-consuming revenge against Professor Moriarty. So, unconscious qualities that Jefferson Hope embodies here do later turn up even in

Holmes's conscious behavior, without, however, revealing their roots. (For an aesthetic rather than a psychological look at the dynamics of Holmes's self-consuming revenge against Moriarty, see the chapter on "The Final Problem.")

8. As the canon unfolds, we can observe Watson's increasingly important role as a bearer of the feeling function, reacting against Holmes's indifference to emotion. He brings to his later narratives stronger and more consistent feelings about suffering, injustice, and even love. (In the very next novel, *The Sign of Four,* Watson falls in love in such a way that the success of his romance depends on the failure of Holmes's rational scheme to restore a treasure to Mary Morstan; Watson's feeling succeeds because Holmes's thinking fails.)

9. Synoptic comments by Freud on the oceanic feeling and subsequent differentiations may be found in the opening chapters of *Civilization and Its Discontents*. Erich Neumann, Jung's favored student, offers the most comprehensive and detailed account in *The Origins and History of Consciousness*, especially sections A of part 1 and part 2. (The later move that saints and mystics make toward a conscious return to oceanic oneness is beyond the scope of Holmes's adventuring, as also indicated in the yogic analysis in the chapter on "The Speckled Band.")

10. *The Valley of Fear,* like *A Study in Scarlet,* features a second part set in America and told by a voice not entirely like that of the first section. But its purpose and status are quite different from those in part 2 of *A Study in Scarlet*. Using in his last novel one of the features of his first, Doyle has become more self-conscious as a writer. He has Watson take pains, when he initially departs from his firsthand narrative in part 1, chapter 3, to beg his readers' leave for using a synopsis, presumably based largely on the accounts of those he meets at the scene of the crime, as the most efficient and evocative way of narrating. And when Watson prepares to take a more pronounced and prolonged leave from the narrative mode of the frame tale in part 2, he again begs the reader's indulgence, explicitly promising that the second narrative will clarify the first for everyone. Further, he claims authorship of the second part as his own, though seeding the case with a strong hint that his information comes from the narrative written while in hiding by the principal of the tale, Birdy Edwards (aka John Douglas and John McMurdo). And though the second part of *The Valley of Fear* is written with less urbanity than the first, bathos is generally avoided; it is in a style that Watson would at least not be embarrassed to own, nor Holmes to read. In the epilogue to the tale there is every indication that Holmes is familiar with the contents of part 2 and finds them of interest, since they relate

strongly (if a little mechanically) to the machinations of Moriarty. And Edwards, far from being a shadowy opposite to Holmes, is in fact a detective himself, able to don disguises and suppress emotions in the cause of his work. (Later, Holmes even emulates Edwards's strategies when he joins incognito an Irish-American terrorist organization in "His Last Bow.")

In fact, so far is the later text from the rough and ready (though revealing) amalgamation of narratives that comprise *A Study in Scarlet* that writing itself seems to be a central feature of its concern. In *The Valley of Fear,* not only do we have Watson's careful easing of the reader from one section of the tale to another in contrast to the almost oracular intrusion in the first novel, but we are faced with a host of motifs that bear directly on writing. The principals of the frame tale remark on the fact that it is their destiny to appear in one of Watson's narratives; Holmes casts himself as a dramatist; and there are chapters with such self-consciously literary titles as "The Tragedy of Birlstone" and "The People of the Drama." The first Scowrer crime in which Edwards is involved is an assault on a newspaper editor, whom he alone prevents from being killed; the profession he attributes to the detective rumored to be investigating the Scowrers (in fact himself) is that of a newspaper reporter; and finally, while the English investigators are attempting to unravel the present crime, Edwards is secretly producing a manuscript that will clarify and justify the events at Birlstone. This pervasive concern with the niceties of writing and the careful integration of both halves of the narrative distinguish the structure of Conan Doyle's last novel from his first, though we may in the end prefer the earlier, less polished, less conscious work as the more compelling of the two.

CHAPTER 5

1. Even today, the mystery of money is that this seeming opposite to soul is so richly connected to our soul's life, so that to speak of one is to suggest the other. Think how many key words psychology and economics share: interest, principle, bond, safe, duty, share, investment, change. Such coincidences are no coincidence. In the very roots of our language, money is connected to the power of psyche, if we will but remember. Money, of course, is at root a substitute for memory, an easier way of keeping account of who owes what to whom. In ancient times, money was more than a medium of exchange because memory was not just a useful mental faculty, but sacred—the mother of all the

soul's Muses. In Greek her name is *Mnemosyne;* in Latin, *Moneta*—the root of our words for money, a strong hint that rather than being the enemy of psyche, money is deeply connected to it. *Moneta* was an epithet for Juno, in whose temple Roman money was minted, which links money to the mother—to *mater* as well as matter, to the feminine, even the domestic. *Moneta* is itself derived from *moneo*—to remind, to recollect, to warn, to teach—and the root of *moneo* is *mens,* the name of the Roman goddess of thought, originally the feminine noun for mind, heart, soul, later narrowed to designate rationality, as in the Mensa Society. So both contemporary and historical language remind us that our fantasies about money are linked to our reflections about our minds, our souls. See Russell A. Lockhart, "Coins and Psychological Change," 18–20, and James Hillman, "A Contribution to Soul and Money," 31–43, in Lockhart, *Soul and Money.*

2. Much of the reflexive discomfort with which some critics view literary deconstruction arises because its principle of *différance* is closely related to exchange's endless chain of substitution.

3. Holmes typically discounts the political dimensions of existence and shows that mysteries that look political in fact are not. When the detective opines that the smashed busts of Napoleon have nothing to do with anarchy or that the socialist slogan "Rache" scrawled in blood on the wall is a decoy in a strictly personal crime, Conan Doyle's plots show him to be correct.

4. In fact, that was exactly Conan Doyle's strategy when he tired of Holmes and tried to get rid of him in "The Final Problem." There, he pitted Holmes in a death struggle with Professor Moriarty, "the organizer of half that is evil and of nearly all that is undetected in this great city," and the resulting battle eliminated them both—until Conan Doyle was forced to bring Holmes back a few years later to please a demanding public and fill a thinning wallet. I deal at length with Holmes's disappearance in the chapter on "The Final Problem."

5. For an extended reflection on strategies for responding to the formulaic qualities in formula stories, see chapter 9 on "The Six Napoleons."

CHAPTER 6

1. Freud wrote these with Breuer and published them in 1893–95. "A Case of Identity" was published in 1891.

2. Published two years after "A Case of Identity."

3. In that tale Holmes also mentions, with a flourish, that there are twenty-three other characteristics of the fragment that further reveal its source. In the spirit of inventiveness and good humor, commentator John Ball Jr. has taken up the challenge and listed/concocted twenty-three more salient characteristics of the signifier—from the rag content of the paper to the presence or absence of erasures and the right- or left-handedness of the writers—very much in the semiotic spirit of Holmes's investigation (see *The Annotated Sherlock Holmes*, 1:343).

4. J. E. Cirlot's *Dictionary of Symbols*, 182–85, presents an interesting overview and bibliography.

5. Despite Jacques Derrida's cogent and intriguing critique of this hierarchy in *Of Grammatology* and elsewhere, it remains the common-sense view that speech is fuller of presence than writing. And so it is here. Still, inversions that suggest a Derridean reordering of the traditional hierarchy of presence can be found in this story. Windibank's need to type the letters rests on the assumption that "even the smallest sample" of his familiar handwriting would risk revealing him in a way that his physical presence and voice would not, if these were disguised. Presumably his character was so thoroughly ingrained in his handwriting that it could not be disguised.

6. The phrase is Morris Berman's. See his excellent book *The Reenchantment of the World* for his contention that the empiricists only disenchanted experience, a view I take some issue with here.

7. Charles Higham, *Adventures of Conan Doyle*, 61.

8. Higham, 143.

9. Higham, 63.

CHAPTER 7

1. *The Annotated Sherlock Holmes*, 2:132.

2. *Spurs*, 51. Throughout this book, Derrida uses a shifting series of relationships between images of women and philosophical truth. All the quotations I use here are drawn from the discussion spanning pages 48–53.

CHAPTER 8

1. Higham, 114.

2. By this point in the chapter, you may well be wondering where the usual summary of the story at hand might be. And alerted by the

absence of the usual epigraphs to mark each section of this chapter, you might well begin to wonder if I, too, have been taken over by the aesthetics of absence. Only partly. Though the paragraphs immediately following are intended to show how this story inverts the usual paradigm, they also provide a quick review of its events.

3. *The Poetics of Prose*, 44, 47.

CHAPTER 9

1. Charles Higham, *The Adventures of Conan Doyle*, 180–81.

2. Once Conan Doyle took up the Holmes stories again, he at first wrote them prolifically, publishing more than a dozen in the next sixteen months and collecting them in 1905 as *The Return of Sherlock Holmes*. His previous collections had set a standard of twelve tales to the book, but here Conan Doyle added a thirteenth, "The Adventure of the Second Stain," to make it a Baker Street dozen. In the added tale, the last in the volume, Conan Doyle pointedly has Watson mention that Holmes has "definitely retired." And indeed, Conan Doyle published no new Holmes stories until 1908, and then only intermittently. His novel *The Valley of Fear* was serialized in 1914 and 1915, and other stories appeared sporadically until ten seemed enough to collect in 1917 as *His Last Bow,* another promise of finality inscribed in its title. All the adventures in that collection were set before Holmes's retirement, except for the title story, in which Holmes returns to detection to support the British war effort. Over the next ten years, Conan Doyle averaged just over one Holmes story a year, collecting the final dozen in 1927 as *The Case Book of Sherlock Holmes* three years before his death. He was often at the point of taking his hero off the stage, fearing in the end that "Mr. Sherlock Holmes may become like one of those popular tenors who, having outlived their time, are still tempted to make repeated farewell bows to their indulgent audiences." But Conan Doyle could never quite leave off repeating the formula he worked so well, and in the end he seems to have reconciled himself to continuing the stories. In the preface to *The Case Book* he tells his readers that he originally determined

> to bring Holmes to an end, as I felt that my literary energies
> should not be directed too much into one channel. . . . [Yet] I
> have never regretted [bringing him back], for I have not in
> actual practice found that these lighter sketches have prevented
> me from exploring and finding my limitations in such varied
> branches of literature as history, poetry, historical novels, psychic

research, and the drama. Had Holmes never existed I could not have done more, though [Conan Doyle adds, with only a trace of chagrin] he may perhaps have stood a little in the way of the *recognition* of my more serious literary work. [my emphasis]

3. Samuel Rosenberg's *Naked Is the Best Disguise* is one of the most audacious books ever written on Holmes. Rosenberg proposes that the Holmes stories constitute a veritable *canon à clef*, with all major and many minor characters corresponding to significant historical figures. He identifies Professor Moriarty as Professor Friedrich Nietzsche and makes Sherlock Holmes into Jesus Christ. I intend no such allegory, but only argue for the presence in this story of several Nietzschean ideas that had achieved popular currency among English writers and intellectuals, ideas that would have special reason to appeal to Conan Doyle at this juncture in his career.

4. Also titled *The Gay Science*, in *The Portable Nietzsche*, 93–94.

5. There is, in fact, a third model for the artist in the story— Beppo, craftsman and criminal, who like Conan Doyle pushes a pearl into a piece of mass-produced art, a treasure that becomes evident only when the familiar, conventional visage is shattered.

6. Nietzsche borrowed the term "Übermensch" from Goethe's *Faust*. It has often been translated as "Superman," a word that has acquired too many overtones from popular culture to be used safely these days; hence, "Overman."

7. The term is also sometimes translated "revaluation," which has the disadvantage of resembling the more cautious, judicious "reevaluation."

8. This resembles Jung's idea that when we revisit problems in our lives, we do so not in a vicious circle but in a spiral, encountering a problem at different levels of experience and integration.

9. See J. P. Stern's succinct analysis of this passage in *Friedrich Nietzsche*, 156–57.

10. Beppo is not the only criminal Holmes emulates. Carrying the photograph of Beppo that he took from the murdered Pietro Venucci's pocket and showing it to those he meets on his trail, Holmes follows the dead mafioso's method in his own search for Beppo.

11. Like the deeply contradictory and fascinating Napoleon, now republican and now emperor, who both codified the law and broke it extravagantly, Holmes has a complex relation to legality.

WORKS CITED

Avalon, Arthur (Sir John Woodroffe). *The Serpent Power: The Secrets of Tantric and Shaktic Yoga.* New York: Dover, 1953.

Baring-Gould, William S., ed. *The Annotated Sherlock Holmes.* By Sir Arthur Conan Doyle. 2 vols. New York: Clarkson N. Potter, 1967.

Barthes, Roland. *Mythologies.* Trans. Annette Lavers. New York: Hill and Wang, 1972.

———. *The Pleasure of the Text.* Trans. Richard Miller. New York: Hill and Wang, 1975.

———. *S/Z.* Trans. Richard Miller. New York: Hill and Wang, 1974.

Bate, Walter Jackson. *The Burden of the Past and the English Poet.* Cambridge: Harvard University Press, 1970.

Berman, Morris. *The Reenchantment of the World.* Ithaca: Cornell University Press, 1981.

Bloom, Harold. *The Anxiety of Influence.* New York: Oxford University Press, 1981.

———. *Kabbalah and Criticism.* New York: Seabury, 1975.

———. *A Map of Misreading.* New York: Oxford University Press, 1975.

———. *Poetry and Repression.* New Haven: Yale University Press, 1976.

Brown, Norman O. *Life against Death.* New York: Vintage, 1959.

Burke, Kenneth. *Counter-Statement.* Berkeley and Los Angeles: University of California Press, 1968.

Campbell, Joseph. *The Hero with a Thousand Faces.* Princeton: Princeton University Press, 1972.

———. *The Mythic Image.* Princeton: Princeton University Press, 1974.

Cawelti, John G. *Adventure, Mystery, and Romance: Formula Stories as Art and Popular Culture.* Chicago: University of Chicago Press, 1976.

Cirlot, J. E. *Dictionary of Symbols.* New York: Philosophical Library, 1971.

Culler, Jonathan. *Ferdinand de Saussure.* New York: Penguin, 1977.

———. *On Deconstruction.* Ithaca: Cornell University Press, 1982.

Derrida, Jacques. *Of Grammatology.* Trans. Gayatri Chakravorty Spivak. Baltimore: Johns Hopkins University Press, 1974.

Derrida, Jacques. *Positions.* Trans. Alan Bass. Chicago: University of Chicago Press, 1981.

————. *Spurs: Nietzsche's Styles.* Trans. Barbara Harlow. Chicago: University of Chicago Press, 1979.

Dove, George N. *Suspense in the Formula Story.* Bowling Green, Ohio: Bowling Green State University Popular Press, 1989.

Doyle, Arthur Conan. *The Complete Sherlock Holmes.* Garden City, N.Y.: Doubleday, 1930.

Eagleton, Terry. *Criticism and Ideology.* London: Verso, 1978.

————. *Literary Theory: An Introduction.* Minneapolis: University of Minnesota Press, 1983.

————. *Marxism and Literary Criticism.* Berkeley and Los Angeles: University of California Press, 1976.

Edwards, Owen Dudley. *The Quest for Sherlock Holmes.* New York: Barnes and Noble, 1983.

Freud, Sigmund. *Civilization and Its Discontents.* Trans. and ed. James Strachey. New York: Norton, 1962.

Freud, Sigmund, and Josef Breuer. *Studies on Hysteria.* Trans and ed. James Strachey. New York: Basic Books, 1957.

Frye, Northrop. *Anatomy of Criticism.* New York: Atheneum, 1957.

————. *The Secular Scripture: A Study of the Structure of Romance.* Cambridge: Harvard University Press, 1976.

Hanh, Thich Nhat. *Old Path White Clouds: Walking in the Footsteps of the Buddha.* Berkeley: Parallax, 1991.

Hassan, Ihab. *The Postmodern Turn.* Columbus: Ohio State University Press, 1987.

Hawkes, Terence. *Structuralism and Semiotics.* London: Methuen, 1977.

Higham, Charles. *Adventures of Conan Doyle.* Norton: New York, 1976.

Hillman, James. *Re-Visioning Psychology.* New York: Harper, 1977.

Holland, Norman. *Poems in Persons.* New York: Norton, 1973.

Jung, Carl G. *Aion: Phenomenology of the Self.* Princeton: Princeton University Press, 1959. Also easily found in *The Portable Jung.* Ed. Joseph Campbell. New York: Viking, 1971. And in *Psyche and Symbol.* Ed. Violet S. de Laszlo. New York: Doubleday Anchor, 1958.

————. *Four Archetypes.* Trans. R. F. C. Hull. Princeton: Princeton University Press, 1970.

————. *Man and His Symbols.* Ed. John Freeman. New York: Dell, 1964.

————. *Mysterium Conjunctionis.* Trans. R. F. C. Hull. Princeton: Princeton University Press, 1977.

————. *Symbols of Transformation.* Trans. R. F. C. Hull. Princeton: Princeton University Press, 1976.

Klossowski de Rola, Stanislas. *Alchemy: The Secret Art.* New York: Avon, 1973.

Lacan, Jacques. "Seminar on 'The Purloined Letter.'" In *The Purloined Poe: Lacan, Derrida, and Psychoanalytic Reading.* Ed. John P. Muller and William J. Richardson. Baltimore: Johns Hopkins University Press, 1988: 28–54. Originally published in English in *French Freud: Structural Studies in Psychoanalysis, Yale French Studies* 48 (1972): 39–72.

Leitch, Vincent. *Deconstructive Criticism: An Advanced Introduction.* New York: Columbia University Press, 1983.

Lévi-Strauss, Claude. *The Savage Mind.* Trans. George Weidenfeld. Chicago: University of Chicago Press, 1966.

———. *Totemism.* Trans. Rodney Needham. New York: Penguin, 1969.

Lockhart, Russell, et al. *Soul and Money.* Dallas: Spring, 1982.

Meyer, Nicholas. *The Seven-Percent Solution.* New York: Dutton, 1974.

Neuman, Erich. *The Origins and History of Consciousness.* Trans. R. F. C. Hull. Princeton: Princeton University Press, 1971.

Nietzsche, Friedrich. *The Gay Science (The Joyful Wisdom), The Twilight of the Idols,* and *Ecce Homo.* In *The Portable Nietzsche.* Ed. and trans. Walter Kaufmann. New York: Viking, 1954.

———. *The Will to Power.* Trans. Walter Kaufmann and R. J. Hollingdale. Ed. Walter Kaufmann. New York: Random House, 1967.

Norris, Christopher. *Deconstruction: Theory and Practice.* London: Methuen, 1982.

O'Hara, Daniel, ed. *Why Nietzsche Now?* Bloomington: Indiana University Press, 1985.

Redmond, Christopher. *In Bed with Sherlock Holmes.* Toronto: Simon and Pierre, 1984.

Rosenberg, Samuel. *Naked Is the Best Disguise: The Death and Resurrection of Sherlock Holmes.* New York: Bobbs-Merrill, 1974.

Sengstan. *Hsin Hsin Ming: Verses on the Faith Mind.* Trans. Richard B. Clarke. In *Teachings of the Buddha.* Ed. Jack Kornfield. Boston: Shambhala, 1993. Also translated as "On Believing in Mind" in *Manual of Zen Buddhism.* Trans. and ed. D. T. Suzuki. New York: Grove, 1960.

Shankara. *Crest-Jewel of Discrimination (Viveka-Chudamani).* Trans. Swami Prabhavananda and Christopher Isherwood. Hollywood, Calif.: Vedanta Press, 1975, 90–91.

Stern, J. P. *Friedrich Nietzsche.* Penguin: New York, 1978.

Suzuki, Shunryu. *Zen Mind, Beginner's Mind.* New York: Weatherhill, 1970.

Todorov, Tzvetan. *The Poetics of Prose.* Trans. Richard Howard. Ithaca: Cornell University Press, 1977.

Tracy, Jack. *The Encyclopaedia Sherlockiana*. Garden City, N.Y.: Doubleday, 1977.

von Franz, Marie-Louise. *Patterns of Creativity Mirrored in Creation Myths*. Dallas: Spring, 1986.

―――. *Shadow and Evil in Fairy Tales*. Dallas: Spring, 1987.

von Franz, Marie-Louise, and James Hillman. *Jung's Typology*. Dallas: Spring, 1971.

Wall, Wayne. *God and Sherlock Holmes: A Study in the Life and Literature of Arthur Conan Doyle*. West Columbia, S.C.: The Hansom Wheels, 1984.